HOLY SPIRITS!

CHARLESTON CULTURE THROUGH COCKTAILS

HOLY SPIRITS!

CHARLESTON CULTURE THROUGH COCKTAILS

Taneka Reaves & Johnny Caldwell

EVENING POST BOOKS

To the Believers and the Dreamers, for Never Accepting "NO" as the Answer.

Published by
Evening Post Books
Charleston, South Carolina

Copyright © 2018 The Post and Courier
All rights reserved.
First edition

Editor: John M. Burbage
Designer: Gill Guerry
Cover photo: Jovon Roberts

Photography: All images by Jovon Roberts unless otherwise noted.

First printing 2018
Printed in the United States of America

A CIP catalog record for this book has been applied
for from the Library of Congress.

ISBN: 978-1-929647-35-4

Although the authors and publisher have made every effort to ensure that the information in this book is correct at time of publication, the authors and publisher do not assume and hereby disclaim any liability to any party for any loss, damage or disruption caused by errors or omissions, whether such errors or omissions result from negligence, accident, or any other cause.

The information in this book is meant for entertaining purposes and to supplement, not replace, proper bar training. Before practicing the skills described in this book, be sure that your equipment is well maintained, and do not take risks beyond your level of experience, aptitude, training and comfort level.

Consumption and use of alcohol poses some inherent risk. The authors and publisher advise readers to take full responsibility for their safety and know their limits. According to the Surgeon General, women should not drink alcoholic beverages during pregnancy because of the risk of birth defects. Consumption of alcoholic beverages impairs your ability to drive a car or operate machinery, and may cause health problems. The legal drinking age in the United States is 21 years old. For the safety of yourself and others, do not drink and drive. Please drink responsibly and take #GentleLadySips.

Whitney –
Thanks for joining
our virtual mixology
session with Ryan
White Wellness.
Here's to living
your best life!
Cheers!
Johnny 2021

Whitney!
thank you so much
for your support! Hope you
enjoy the stories & the cocktails
in this book!

Cheers!
Amelia
T. Peacock
2021

TABLE OF CONTENTS

PREFACE

Spreading the Gospel of the Cocktail Bandits.................................... 13

FOREWORD

On the 8th day, God said: 'I think I'll have a drink!'........................... 15

CHAPTER 1

What's a Charleston Cocktail?... 19

Building a Home Bar... 31

CHAPTER 2

Sisters in Sips — How love of tequila, adventure sparked a social media movement ... 41

A Bandit Toast — To getting by with help from friends........................... 48

CHAPTER 3

Port of Rum — Imported slaves, sugar fueled the city's economy.................. 55

Liquor, Beer and Ales — Charleston is known for holding its own................. 58

Holy Mixers & Wine... 67

Southern Hospitality — Entertaining tips from the Bandit Belles................. 71

Gullah Cuisine — African-American food clears heads, brings people together..... 74

CHAPTER 4

Holy Spirits! Recipes (see list on next page).................................. 80

About the Cocktail Bandits.. 167

References.. 170

Terminology... 172

Acknowledgments... 173

Special Thanks To:.. 174

RECIPES

Vodka

Peninsula Tea 85

Afro Alchemy 86

Barnfly. 87

Fresh Blush. 88

Fire Flying on the Island. 91

The Blonde Reaper. 92

Grapefruit Bliss 95

Hibiscus Chucktown Mule 96

Tequila

Phoenix. 99

Foxtrap .100

Blacker the Berry 103

Tequila (cont.)

Porgy & Bess 104
Bandita Amor 106
Chucktown Frozen Strawberry Margarita . . .106
Family Portrait 107
Port of Coupes 107
Dill — With It 108
La Bandita Lagerita 111

Rum

Skywalker 112
Black Girl Magic 114
Rum Day Cap 114
Spice and Everything Nice 115
One in a Mellon 117

Gin

Thunder Garden 118
Cabin Fever 120
Glass Door 123
Gentle Lady Gimlet 124
Party Line 127
Charleston Single 128
Power Suit 130
The Blue Bully 133
Flower Crown 134
Lady in Red 137
Living La Vida Local 138

Bourbon

Upstate Revival 141
The Ginger Lady 142
New Charleston Sour 142
Pama Paradise 143
Lowcountry Sunsets 144

Specialty

Carolina Shandy 147
Morning Glory 148
The Legendary Porter 150

Mocktails

Magnolia Song 151
Virgin Grapefruit Sour 151
Blue Whale 152
Grandma's Sweet Tea 155

Guest Cocktails

A Place in Thyme — Jeremiah Schenzel . . .156
Against the Grain — Allen Lancaster 159
Freedom of Peach — Megan Deschaine . . .160
Queen of Kings — Rochelle Jones 163
Mexican Compromise — Ramon Caraballo .165

PREFACE
Spreading the Gospel of the Cocktail Bandits

What you're holding right now is a handful of delight — a book featuring just the right blend of history, humor and photographs with a kick: an introduction to historic Charleston and the up-and-coming art of true Southern mixology. The goal is to inspire you to research and experiment with different flavors that combine to make excellent drinks with alcohol — or without, if you so choose — and to excite your best senses again and again.

You'll have a hard time finding anyone more passionate about sharing their love of craft cocktails than Johnny Caldwell and Taneka Reaves. The two South Carolinians befriended each other at the College of Charleston 15 years ago and have been enjoying life ever since. They are the Cocktail Bandits. Their mission is to educate, empower and entertain.

They built their blog in 2013 to showcase their adventures in Charleston's ever-evolving culinary industry and to use the powers of their vivacious personalities and social media to grow an international audience of cocktail enthusiasts. Today they have nearly 30,000 followers in the United States. The Cocktail Bandits continue to expand their knowledge of the beverage and entertainment industry by attending niche conferences, hosting social media seminars and staging unique parties featuring great music and live cocktail demonstrations.

The duo travels primarily in the Southeastern region of the United States spreading the gospel of Charleston — also known as the Holy City — and their deep appreciation of mixed drinks. And they have only just begun. To paraphrase Mr. Shakespeare, the world is their oyster (with either gin or vodka, vermouth and an olive) and the pearl is to make the perfect mix.

COCKTAIL BANDITS

The old Pink House Tavern still stands on Chalmers Street.

FOREWORD
On the 8th day, God said: 'I think I'll have a drink!'

After Charleston's first settlers found work, they secured housing for their families, built places of worship for their souls, and sought communal space for open discussion and good libations. Not much along those lines has changed.

The home, of course, is where the heart is and houses went up on deep, narrow lots soon after Charles Town was founded in 1670. Churches did too — lots of them. A desire for religious freedom prompted many European families of various faiths to risk everything and start a new life in the new city named in honor of England's King Charles II.

Developing this "New World" was a challenge almost beyond what anyone could imagine, and those who undertook it for whatever reasons relied heavily on their God to get them through. Thus, sanctuaries of all major faiths today adorn the streets of the "Holy City" and continue to coexist harmoniously.

Indeed, Charleston has always been a "spirited" place. The circa-1700 Pink House at 17 Chalmers Street is one of the oldest buildings still standing in city. The three-story structure's walls were made of pink coral stone imported from Bermuda. It was first operated as a "groggerie" — with, perhaps, a bordello on the top floor — primarily for visiting sailors. Grog was a mixture of rum and water sprinkled with spices for added flavor. This rather classless drink is considered the first popular Charleston cocktail.

But much has changed since the first spirits were served in the Holy City, and for this the imbibers of Charleston are also very thankful. So, in celebration of our good fortune, homegrown authors Johnny Caldwell and Taneka Reaves — also known as the Cocktail Bandits — give you the book *Holy Spirits! Charleston Culture Through Cocktails*.

Cheers!

— **Victoria Rae Moore**

Victoria Rae Moore is a writer, philanthropist and owner of Victoria Rae Public Relations. She studied classical ballet at Charleston County School of the Arts and graduated with a degree in journalism and mass communications from the University of South Carolina.

"SO PLEASE JOIN US. RAISE A GLASS AS WE OFFER A SPIRITED TOAST TO OUR CURIOUSLY DIVERSE AND HISTORIC PLACE. CHEERS TO THE HOLY CITY! MAY IT STEAL YOUR HEARTS AS IT HAS CAPTURED OUR OWN."

The official tie of the United States Bartenders' Guild. We are on the board of membership and special events.

CHAPTER 1
What's a Charleston cocktail?

C harleston, S.C. is the Cocktail Bandits' town, our stomping ground, where we work and play. So please join us. Raise a glass as we offer a spirited toast to our curiously diverse and historic place. Cheers to the Holy City! May it steal your hearts as it has captured our own.

Neither of us are formally trained bartenders, but we do enjoy having a good drink. Taneka first worked as a server in a few taverns beyond the city limits, but she could not land the food-service job she wanted downtown. Meanwhile Johnny, a new law-school graduate, was told again and again she was not experienced enough to join a prestigious Broad Street firm and overqualified for alternative legal work. So, unemployed, we sat down to figure out what we ought to do, and only after a drink or two, we had committed ourselves to starting a business of our own.

First, we developed a business plan, which to this day remains quite simple: "Know your product, make lots of connections and share Charleston's wealth of spirits specially spiced with our own imagination." Thus, Cocktail Bandits, LLC, was born.

We joined the local chapter of the United States Bartenders' Guild, which was an extremely valuable investment. It connected us with other chapter members throughout the United States. We attended industry-only events hosted by global companies, including Hendrick's Gin and Grand Marnier. Whiskey and sherry seminars led by major brand ambassadors gave us direct interaction with suppliers with whom we continue to collaborate. We also got the opportunity to taste rare and expensive liquors, all in the name of research. What's better than drinking Nolet's Gin with 11th generation distiller Carl Nolet?

We now belong to the Charleston Food and Beverage Collective and love everything about it. This brotherhood and sisterhood of professionals aligned us with almost every bar owner, bartender and liquor representative in Charleston. We quickly established

Ryan Welliver of The Cocktail Club on King Street.

Dave Curry

Companies like Ciroc and Absolut spend big bucks courting bartenders and restaurant owners by vying to become the "house" or "go-to" brand. It's also a great accomplishment to have a particular label listed on the menu as an ingredient in a quality signature cocktail. Indeed, bar staff acquire much data through constant contact with consumers. Good bartenders pick up on current drinking trends like "Rose All Day" and on fads that soon fade. Remember Zima?

Experienced bar staff also introduce new ways to enjoy old favorites. The bar serves as a test kitchen for mixologists who create their own tonics and tinctures with herbs and spices from back porch gardens combined with a little imagination. Innovators like Ryan Welliver are producing botanical shrubs and floral bitters. When you notice smoked vermouth or barrel-aged gin listed among cocktail ingredients, there's a good chance the person behind the bar made it.

relationships visiting fellow guild members at their respective establishments. Each encounter enriched our beverage and business knowledge. We shared images and information about Charleston's cocktail creations on our social media channels, and the word spread like fire.

Competition sparks innovation, so managers of beverage brands look to local bartenders as a unique focus group. They know such mixologists interact daily with consumers. Each customer is engaged at the most critical stage of a transaction: the point of sale. One suggestion from behind the bar can change whether a patron chooses whiskey over vodka, or more importantly, a particular whiskey or a particular vodka. Such exchanges often result in life-long customers. We appreciate that.

The beverage industry loves creativity and searches endlessly for new ways the drinking public can enjoy various products. Cocktail competitions also play a key role in cultivating innovation. Typically, these competitions challenge the bar community to craft a special drink while following a set of broad guidelines. Motivated by a cash prize or an all-expense-paid trip to some exotic place, mixologists pull out all the stops to win.

We've had the honor of judging cocktail competitions. As fun as that sounds, it's no easy feat. It's difficult to choose a winner among so many outstanding drinks (not to mention the more you sip the

The best bars have a great mix of local, national and international spirits.

better they might taste). Often times, we are familiar with the competitors, making the decision process more challenging. We leave competitions impressed and inspired to create even more of our own cocktails.

Communication is key. Proper articulation of one's needs eliminates confusion, clarifies conflict and cures complications. It's a matter of respect. You would never wave money and shout "Hey You!" to your lawyer or dentist, so why would you be rude to your bartender, the one person who can quench your thirst and make you feel at home in a crowd?

Bandit behavior

When drinking the Bandit Way, dress up like you mean it, select a popular establishment during happy hour and, if necessary, wiggle your way through the crowd to a seat at the bar. Note: The bartender will see you even if he or she doesn't make eye contact initially. So, don't make too big of a scene.

If there is a cocktail menu, review it carefully. No need to ask for specials if they are listed. When approached by the bartender, know your order, especially if the establishment is busy. Also keep your questions to a minimum. No one likes indecision when the crowd at the bar is four people deep.

Megan Deschaine is the bar manager at Macintosh, VP of the United States Bartenders' Guild and the Belle Meade Madeira representative.

Happy hours are designed to draw a crowd. Most places offer reduced prices for such a select period of time Monday through Thursday. Take advantage of this and order more than one craft cocktail without seriously damaging your financial assets. Don't feel guilty about ordering a bite or two as appetizers, which are usually discounted as well.

One of our favorite pastimes is taking a visitor out on the town. Most tourist maps and city guides don't highlight places that locals enjoy. We often avoid restaurants that attract too many tourists. That's because service might suffer when employees don't expect return business. "Flipping tables" is the name of that game. This practice encourages customers to order, consume and move on, making room for the next paying customer. Moreover, if you are in the

Jeremiah Schenzel was previously the bar manager at Scarecrow & Co. He is now the owner of DAPS Breakfast & Imbibe.

mood to taste and sample a variety of new spirits, it's nearly impossible to do so among a pack of tourists.

Over the years, we have established relationships with restaurateurs, bar managers, hostesses, bar backs and line cooks. Each plays an integral part in our overall beverage experience. Each individual brings a deep and diverse background into the bar every evening. You'll also find yourself anticipating some light-hearted sarcasm from behind the bar designed to keep the hostesses and guests smiling.

We take advantage of our bonds with area bartenders and other culinary professionals, so we comprised a list of questions for them to answer to provide us with insight regarding their perspectives on Charleston's food and beverages. That list is the basis for this book.

"What is a Charleston cocktail?" we asked, and "Has the drinking culture changed?" and so on and so forth. Each response was duly noted, and they included lots of fascinating information. One observation remained the same: Charleston takes care of her own.

Charleston's inclusive nature is what attracted chef-turned-bar manager Jeremiah Schenzel to the area. He got his start working craft bars on King Street before recently opening Charleston's first tiki bar — South Seas — and now DAPS Breakfast & Imbibe. Jeremiah recalls he was intrigued by the innovation of the booming food-and-beverage community. "People aren't afraid to take risks when it comes to dining experiences," he said. As a craft-cocktail artist, Jeremiah considers flavor over everything and pours what he has learned during his seasoned culinary background into every drink he mixes.

Hotel bars are in a lane all their own having served an essential function from the start. Guests depend on them for shelter from the elements and as a place to rest and regroup. In some areas, a lodging house is the only public establishment for miles, but not all hotels are created equal. Charleston, like most mid-sized cities, has a range of options from inexpensive hostels on Spring Street to the grand and iconic Charleston Place Hotel at King and Market streets that also houses high-end stores, including Gucci and Louis Vuitton, as well as large venue spaces for major conferences and retreats in our city.

Rochelle Jones at Stars Rooftop & Grill Room.

Hotel staffers have extended interactions with guests. Lobby attendants communicate with visitors who are coming and going throughout the day. To welcome weary travelers, fine hotels typically serve light refreshments upon arrival. This creates an interesting dynamic between guests and staff. It allows for the quick development of a relationship. Patrons not only ask for guest services but also request travel recommendations, weather reports and other important information.

Boutique hotel bar manager Allen Lancaster enjoys the intimate connection he has with guests. At The Spectator, a 40-room hotel on State Street, Lancaster enjoys making guests feel at home. "Charleston takes care of its own," he said, "and when you're in Charleston, you're family." His focus is on providing exceptional service while tending bar. "I feel a responsibility to ensure a pleasurable experience during their brief visits in our city," said Allen, a former restaurant owner.

Guests checking into the hotel are greeted with a craft drink. This "welcome" cocktail usually features seasonal fruit and botanical spirits to refresh the new arrivals. Allen is also proud of The Spectator's impressive turndown service. Every evening, guests are treated to a spirited shot of goodness in the form of a chocolate bite left on their pillows. Other area hotels host a complimentary happy hour, offering libations and light snacks in their lobby areas. If you make people feel at home, they never want to leave.

Bar pros

A firm believer in entrepreneurship, Rochelle Jones has taken her food and beverage career to an even higher level. She designs and sells a signature line of cocktail infusions. Using unique and sometimes rare ingredients including bison grass and hibiscus, Jones has given bartenders a range of Southern flavors to play with. Her "Southern Twist" brand offers easy-to-serve, low-calorie, non-alcoholic mixers.

Rochelle is found most days behind the bar at Stars Rooftop & Grill Room on King Street crafting cocktails and pouring wine from 16 imports on tap. She encourages women in the industry to pursue ways to grow within the profession. "There are lots of opportunities to be more than just a pretty face behind the bar," she said. "Women bring with them different perspectives and palettes. More ladies behind the bar equals more floral, less aggressively spirited cocktails.

Native to Charleston, Megan Deschaine is thrilled by the city's growing craft cocktail market. It is consistently listed as the best small city to visit in the world by publications such as Travel + Leisure and Conde Nast magazines. Meg contributes to her love for the city through curated beverages and by build-

Allen Lancaster of Spectator Hotel making cocktails with High Wire's Sorghum Whiskey.

ing cocktails in front of customers as part of their drinking experience. The Macintosh, also on King Street, serves as her stage as she creates cocktails according to the season. Bar patrons enjoy watching all the steps and skills required to assemble their beverages. The show is included in the drink price, so enjoy a little flair in her presentations.

Deschaine recommends that all new bartenders find a mentor. Often times, servers are hired and soon placed behind the bar without proper training. It's baptism by fire as a new member of the wait staff is forced to learn crafting techniques while on the job. Partnering with a good mentor can be the difference between a bad summer waiting tables or

Evan Christy making a Holy Spirits cocktail.

Coupe glasses are perfect for cocktails and bubbly!

a long, profitable career in the food and beverage industry. Meg credits her friend and mentor Doug Atwell, owner of The Rye Bar in Washington, D.C., for her passion for and knowledge of the profession.

Ramon Caraballo, head bartender at The Rarebit on King Street, keeps his taste buds focused on the future. His bar boasts a late-night menu that serves urban hipsters and techies alike. He has witnessed an increase in orders for tequila, Amaros and Spiritz Liquor. Caraballo attributes Charleston's warm climate for the desire for refreshing light cocktails that one can sip on a patio all day long. His bar serves Moscow Mules on tap using ginger beer and tonic soda crafted by one of his fellow bartenders. Ramon finds himself sipping from the signature copper cups after every shift.

Caraballo chooses to unwind at local watering holes including the Recovery Room on King Street. He enjoys convening with other bar professionals in a comfortable environment. There's a mutual respect among service industry workers that is clearly witnessed in dive bars after 12 a.m. This space to congregate and commiserate is great for building relationships among Charleston's growing food and beverage community.

Cocoa Rae

The Mexican Compromise, made by Ramon Caraballo, is stirred. Stirred cocktails are more booze forward than shaken cocktails.

Cocoa Rae

The Mexican Compromise Cocktail from Rarebit. They have the best glassware.

Building a home bar

Charleston has a long tradition of home entertaining. Since settlement in 1670, residents of all statuses enjoyed hosting guests. The first rule for becoming a proper hostess is to ensure that no one goes hungry or thirsty while under your roof. Keep your fridge stocked with go-to appetizers and your bar full of quality spirits, liqueurs, cordials, syrups and more.

Building a bar at home is the new "it" thing! The task isn't nearly as intimidating or expensive as it may seem. There are a few tools and items that are building blocks for an amazing home bar and for producing delicious craft cocktails to serve from it. Check out the following categories:

Alcohol
Mixers
Bar Tools
Glassware
Garnishes

Alcohol comes first. After all, it is the main attraction. And no good bar is missing quality bottles of vodka, gin, Bourbon, rum and tequila.

Vodka

Vodka is a tasteless and odorless spirit made from grains, and it is the most popular and versatile liquor for mixed drinks. It is also used for infusions, tinctures and liqueurs because it delivers flavors with ease.

Tequila

Tequila is our favorite spirit. It comes in five styles: Blanco/Silver, Gold, Reposado, Anejo and extra Anejo. Silver (or white) tequila is the best to mix with cocktails because it is not aged and has only basic agave (spiny leaves on a single stalk with flower clusters) characteristics. It goes great with margaritas and Palomas. Just make sure it's 100 percent agave. (Mixtos, a type of tequila made from fermented agave juice and glucose and fructose sugars, are not fit for cocktails…or even consumption.) Reposados, which are aged from two to 11 months, are also used to make premium cocktails, while Anejo and extra Anejo are aged a year or longer — better when sipped.

Gin

Gin is a multigrain spirit flavored with juniper and botanicals. The main requirement for a good gin is a "piney" flavor. Gin has been served in bars since the 18th century and is the spirit ingredient to make classic cocktails including The Last Word, Gin Rickey and Gin Fizz.

Bourbon

Bourbon. Oh Bourbon! You must have Bourbon whiskey in your home bar. It is the American spirit, distilled from at least 51 percent corn and aged in

new, charred oak barrels. You can make Bourbon anywhere in the United States, but Kentucky lays claim to having the best. Bourbon also has a home here in Charleston where it is beloved by many Southerners.

Scotch

Scotch whisky is the most regulated spirit in the world. It's made only in Scotland from grains (mostly malted barley) and matured there for three years in oak casts as well. It's sold in several forms: Malt whisky is bottled in Scotland. Single malt whisky is distilled from malted barley at a single distillery. Blended whisky is a mix of single malts along with grain alcohol. For whisky tasting, it's best to be served neat. (Trivia: Scots drop the "e" in "whiskey.")

Cordial/liqueur

A liqueur, or cordial, is a sweetened distilled spirit that is as important to cocktail making as are basic liquors. They add more flavor to drinks, and most are below 40 percent ABV (alcohol by volume). The most versatile cordials/liqueurs for a home bar are Cointreau, St. Germaine and Luxardo.

Cointreau is an orange liqueur — basically an expensive triple-sec — that tastes amazing in margaritas and similar drinks. St. Germaine is an elderflower liqueur often referred to as "bartender's ketchup" because it is so versatile. Luxardo is a maraschino liqueur used in classic cocktails.

Beer, Wine

Some guests don't drink "hard liquor." No worries. Have a few beer and wine options in your bar — which simply isn't a bar without a good brew. Local is best. A good Coast Kolsch or a Gullah Cream Ale from Revelry work perfectly. Simple red or white California wines should satisfy wine-loving guests.

Bitters

Bitters are liquor-based flavoring agents used for many things, including an enhancement for cocktails and clearing up stomach ailments. (Seriously!)

The most popular are Angostura Bitters from the islands of Trinidad and Tobago. If local is preferred, Jack Rudy Cocktail Co. has amazing bitters in its inventory. Bitters are the "salt and pepper" of drinks. A few drops will make a cocktail pop with flavor.

Mixers

Now that we have covered the boozy ingredients for the home bar, it's time to move on to mixers, which are non-alcoholic beverages used for "mocktails" and cocktails. They include sodas, juices, syrups, energy drinks and other non-alcoholic beverages.

Soft drinks are perfect for the home bar. Coke, Pepsi, ginger ale, tonic and soda water are the most popular. It's best to buy small bottles or cans because it is less wasteful. Cannonborough Beverage

Co. and O & O Hooch are local and perfect for almost any cocktail.

Juices enhance flavors of a beverage without the carbonation. Common juices for the home bar are pineapple, orange and cranberry.

Syrups

Most cocktails require a sweetener, and syrups are great for amazing drinks. They can be homemade or purchased. The easiest to make is "simple syrup," which consists of equal parts water and sugar boiled until the sugar dissolves. Others include agave syrup, honey syrup and a Southern favorite — sorghum syrup. Get creative to determine which sweetener you like best.

There are a couple of local companies in Charleston that have syrups with incredible flavors: Jack Rudy's Tonic Syrup and Tippleman's Ginger Honey syrup. Remember, a great sweetener almost guarantees a good drink.

Energy Drinks

Let's face it. An energy drink is needed in a home bar. Sometimes a few cocktails, wine or beer make guests lethargic, especially after work. Red Bull is the perfect pick-me-up addition for the bar. Simply add vodka, rum or tequila. But go easy on the Bull!

Fruit/Herbs

Fruits are added to a cocktail for flavor or as a garnish. Important citruses to have on your bar are lemons, limes and oranges.

Herbs are as important as fruit, and mint is the most popular. Basil, sage and thyme are also used as aromatics and garnishes.

Special note on citrus

Citrus fruits — especially lemons and limes — add much needed acidity to cocktails. The tart and tang from the rinds balance an overly sweet or overly spirited cocktail. Keep an array of different citrus options — including grapefruit, tangerines and even pomelos — in your home. Bright-colored juices with natural sweetness reduce the need for artificial sugars. Whenever you can, choose fresh-squeezed juice over store-bought concentrate. Freshly squeezed juice has no added sugar and preservatives, and tastes better too!

Tools for the home bar

We have covered the essential ingredients for a cocktail, so let's consider proper tools needed for your bar. A bartender is only as good as her tools, and having the right equipment will make a cocktail-crafting experience even more enjoyable. Check these out:

Shaker/Mixing tin

There are many mixing tins on the market but the best are Boston shakers and double-tins. The Boston shaker is the most popular in bars and restaurants. It has one tin side and the other side is glass. The glass side is great for stirred cocktails as well. The glass and the tin fit together in such a way that liquid cannot leak when being shaken. The glass side absorbs heat, so, if you want really cold cocktails, use a double-tin. They are also great for creating froth by using egg whites.

Pour spout

Pour spouts are inserted into bottles to provide a smooth, even, stable pour. Pourers assist in the entire cocktail-making process. They are much easier to pour liquid in jiggers as well. But they do clog up, so remember to clean them periodically.

Strainer

Strainers are also necessary for crafting proper cocktails. There are several types of strainer, including the Julep and the Hawthorne. The Hawthorne (pictured lower right) is the most popular.

The Julep is the original cocktail strainer. It is a bowl-shaped metal cup with holes all through it, with a handle. It's not seen often in bars but is an effective tool. It originated in the 1800s so people could enjoy Mint Juleps without dumping ice in their faces. Some say it's the precursor to a straw.

The Hawthorne is the most popular cocktail strainer. These flat disks have a handle, prongs and coiled springs rolled around the bottom that catch solid material from the liquid while making a cocktail. The coils fit most mixing tins and glasses, and the Hawthorne strainer is inexpensive.

A fine-mesh strainer is used when the Hawthorne and Julep strainers need a little help. This strainer removes small pieces of ice, fruit and herbs. It's essentially a second filter for the cocktail. The fine-mesh strainer is essential for a good martini or other cocktail served with no ice.

Bar Spoon

A bar spoon is one of the most valuable tools in the box. It has been around since the initial days of cocktail making and is used for muddling, stirring, mixing, layering and garnishing cocktails quickly and efficiently. Every cocktail does not need to be shaken in a mixing tin. Most booze-forward, classic cocktails are mixed with a spoon.

Knife and cutting board

A knife and cutting board are necessary to cut fruit and herbs for cocktails and garnishes. The sharper the knife the better.

Citrus press, or C-press

The C-press (pictured above, top) is used to squeeze fresh juice out of citrus while retaining seeds and pulp. This tool is handy because it reduces messy clean-up time and prevents the juice from irritating your hand if you have little cuts. Invest $5 in a citrus press to ensure that your home bar is equipped for crafting cocktails with fresh ingredients. After you express the juice, don't discard the rind — it can be peeled and used as a garnish.

Muddler

A muddler is used to smash flavors from herbs and/or fruits. It's great for unique cocktails, and excellent modern-day bartenders use one.

Bottle, can and wine opener

If you serve beer and wine, openers are a no-brainer. Don't forget a can opener for pineapple and apple juice.

Jigger

Jiggers are small tools used to measure liquid. They come in either ounces (oz) or milliliters (ml), and help to ensure exact measurements so that cocktails are consistent and balanced, an essential in making good drinks.

Bar mat

The best bar mats have rubber on the bottom to make mixing easier. Mats assist with spills and other messes that happen when making cocktails. They also keep your shakers, mixing glasses, spoons and jiggers off the bar.

Glassware

Many kinds of glassware have evolved in the world of cocktails. The key is making sure the proper glass is used. There are many reasons that certain drinks are served in particular glasses, and we are going to cover the essentials. This is our advice on best types of glassware for your home bar:

Wines

A red-wine glass has a large bowl to help swirl the wine and allow it to breathe, or "aerate." White-wine glasses have a smaller mouth area, allowing the liquid to have less aeration in the glass. White wine does not need to oxidize as much as red wine; white wine has more delicate notes.

Use a flute glass for champagne. The tall, thin bowl helps preserve bubbles for an extended period of time and the stem is long enough to not be warmed by the hands.

Cocktail glass

This is the quintessential glass for mixed drinks served with or without ice. Its large mouth helps with the aromatic qualities of most traditional cocktails.

Highball glass

A highball glass is used to serve tall cocktails and any drink that requires a lot of mixer. Drinks can either be poured over ice or served as a double-cocktail (sans ice).

Lowball glass

A lowball, or rocks, glass is typical for classic cocktails. It can also be used with drinks that use muddled ingredients. It is the perfect glass for a neat pour of liquor.

"MANY KINDS OF GLASSWARE
HAVE EVOLVED IN THE WORLD OF
COCKTAILS. THE KEY IS MAKING SURE
THE PROPER GLASS IS USED."

"MY GREAT-GRANDMOTHER WAS A
BOOTLEGGER AND MY GRANDFATHER
A DRUNK. I'M SOMEWHERE
IN-BETWEEN."
— **Johnny Caldwell**

CHAPTER 2
Sisters in Sips:
How love of tequila, adventure sparked a social media movement

BY JOHNNY CALDWELL

Charleston is my home, and I knew at a very early age that I wanted to make my family proud. So, I decided to become a lawyer. It seemed as though lawyers were essential to creating change and leading the masses. I also wanted to use my experiences from my legal work to launch a career in politics. All of which is incredibly ambitious for an 8-year-old living in rural Mount Pleasant just east of the Cooper River. I have a long pedigree of socially active and civically minded Southern women in my family.

As children, my siblings and I constantly heard, "Go outside and play." In a way, we were forced to enjoy the warm rays from the sun. We often fed ourselves between meals by picking mulberries and cracking pecans in the backyard. Persimmons, plums and loquats abound in our neighborhood and by the end of each summer, our tongues were blue and our tummies ached.

Many years ago, my great-great-great-great-grandfather Isaiah Wright purchased five acres in what is now called the "Snowden" community. This land remained in our family — passed down from generation to generation. After nearly losing her inheritance due to delinquent taxes, my great-grandmother, Louise Jefferson Brown, paid the overdue bill and built a house there in 1959 for herself and her six children.

Louise was a statuesque woman full of pride, and determined to lead by example and prove the importance of being earnest. I inherited her sense of hard work, appreciation of alcoholic beverages and desire to entertain by way of my DNA.

She operated a speakeasy (Charlestonians call them "blind tigers") from her home, inviting guests in after work to buy beer and stay awhile. She was also known to loan money to those in need — for a fee, of course. In addition, she supported her large and growing family with the income she earned from employment at the old Charleston cigar factory on East Bay Street. Today, the newly renovated facility operates as a prized event venue, luxury condominiums and premium office spaces overlooking the Arthur Ravenel Jr. Bridge over the Cooper River. But in 1960, the factory offered a critical opportunity to the illiterate, single mother of six. Always thinking of her legacy, that house in Mount Pleasant represented security to her descendants. The area was considered "country" back then, and had plenty of space for her to raise her children and, eventually, tend to her grandchildren.

My mother inherited the property from her mother. The remaining property was divided among three immediate family members. Heirs property is a legal tool used to pass on land through generations. Its purpose is to keep property in the family. Unfortunately, uneducated and misinformed residents often face property seizures due to delinquent taxes or by violating local ordinances.

Charleston is fortunate to have a non-profit organization called the Center for Heirs Property, which partners with families to not only legally maintain ownership of their homes but also to profit from natural resources that can be derived from their property.

Fast forward to 2017. My childhood neighborhood is one of the few remaining family-owned, predominately African-American communities in Mount Pleasant, just east of the Ravenel Bridge. This once heavily wooded area now has shopping centers, mega churches, new housing developments, an eight-lane highway and a lot more growth on the way.

Mount Pleasant living boasts waterfront property, award-winning schools and a bustling food and beverage scene, all in close proximity to downtown Charleston. However, with all this development comes higher housing costs and property taxes. Tragically, such growth too often forces families off their land because they can no longer afford it.

I have the privilege of growing up in a family that could afford to purchase and construct a home with access to quality health care, good schools and other advantages in a safe community of like-minded people. I am a product of my environment, surrounded by politically involved women and men, many of whom risked their lives in the defense of our country by serving in the Armed Forces.

But while growing up East of the Cooper River, we rarely ventured across the rickety old John P. Grace Memorial and newer Silas Pearman bridges into downtown Charleston. Constructed in 1929, the two-lane, 20-feet wide, 2.7-mile long Grace Bridge — named after a former Charleston mayor and developer — serviced approximately 35,000 cars and trucks a day before being torn down. This bridge, once considered an engineering marvel, became the

Johnny's great-grandmother, Louise Jefferson Brown.

scariest, most structurally unsound major span in the Southeast. Its "brother" bridge, named after a state highway engineer, was built in 1979 with only three lanes. It wasn't until 2005 that both spans were removed and replaced by the Ravenel Bridge.

We had relatives who lived on peninsular Charleston, but we rarely visited them for fear of crossing the Grace Bridge, which limited my exposure to the economic growth happening mere miles away. It wasn't until I was a freshman at the College of Charleston that I began to understand the significance of the Holy City.

Taneka and I met the first day of college after being invited by mutual friends to a dorm-room party where most of the guests were also incoming freshmen. After an hour or so of dancing to our favorite hip hop tunes, someone suggested we walk down to the historic Charleston Battery. The Battery, which is part of White Point Garden, has been used in defense of the old city for centuries. Today the landmark serves as a public park and popular tourist destination. It is about a mile from the college campus, and on that particular night we were not overly pleased with making the trek in four-inch heels.

Today we say "Yes" to such things. "Yes" is always our answer. Dining out and enjoying life with people is like a sport, and we are the champs. We take every opportunity to visit a new restaurant, museum or art gallery. When invited to grand openings or private receptions, we reply, "Yes." Each event is another opportunity to encounter someone new and experience the thrill of the unknown.

On one such outing, Taneka and I visited the Cocktail Club on King Street for a fun night out. We frequent this location for its exceptional gin cocktails and handsome bartenders. This particular evening the buzz gods treated us extraordinarily well. We sat at a table and were served beautifully garnished cocktails. Then came a bowl of special punch, tequila shots, lime wedges and sweating water glasses. That's because the evening had turned into a major celebration as friends and more friends joined us, ordered round after round and shared great stories.

We were magnetized, it seemed. That's when we realized what was all too clear: We were empowered. We were the Cocktail Bandits!

We purchased a $30 cocktail kit online that included a mixing tin, jigger, bar spoon, basic strainer, a muddler and recipe book. After reading the tips that accompanied the recipe book, we set about crafting. We spent countless hours watching mixology videos, learning bartending basics and perfecting classic cocktail recipes. Step-by-step, we followed the instructions then made modifications using local ingredients. We concocted syrups and tinctures from red cabbage, herbs and other colorful ingredients. Our cocktails reflected our exultant approach to imbibing.

We soon realized that many delicious cocktails were served in Charleston but none represented the city's genuine flavor and soul. We vowed to put Charleston in a glass, allowing folks to drink in what makes our city so special. In the spring of 2015, we were given the opportunity to fulfill our promise.

In April of that year, we received an email from Charleston locals and cookbook authors Matt and Ted Lee, a popular duo of brothers who write on Charleston cuisine and sell their own brand of genuine boiled peanuts.

Big on the festival circuit, the brothers invited us to collaborate with them for a class during Atlanta Food and Wine Festival. They partnered with South Carolina Parks Recreation and Tourism Department to host a seminar on undiscovered state gems such as Carolina Gold rice. We were tasked with creating cocktails using products grown and handcrafted in our home state. Our only requirement was the use of Blenheim Spicy Ginger Ale. The carbonated soda

is brewed in the town of Blenheim, in Dillon County, S.C., near where Taneka was raised. The whole thing was serendipitous.

Delighted to have this opportunity, we began brainstorming what the assignment meant to us. Firefly Spirits quickly came to mind. The company makes Sweet Tea Vodka infused with locally grown leaves. Located near the Firefly distillery on Wadmalaw Island, Charleston Tea Plantation is the only one of its kind in the nation.

The Cocktail Bandits are lifelong sweet-tea lovers as well as proper Southern belles, so we quickly considered what turned out to be the perfect fit. We were familiar with the Tippleman's brand of cocktail syrups from our previous involvement in cocktail competitions. Their Ginger-Honey syrup is incredibly versatile and mixes well with fresh-squeezed lemon juice. We topped the cocktail by adding the spicy soda. Lastly, we garnished the glass with a mint sprig, lemon wheel and a hand-woven Palmetto Rose.

We commissioned Charleston artist Fletcher Williams III to handcraft hundreds of the roses in Gullah-Geechee fashion from Palmetto tree fronds. The weaving of sweetgrass baskets is another cherished tradition passed down from enslaved Africans mostly from areas in and around Sierra Leone. Reed-like sweetgrass plants once grew wild along the Carolina coast, and custom baskets as well as other handmade pieces vary in size and cost. Local, regional and national galleries and museums house large and elaborate sweetgrass creations for their exhibits. Sweetgrass artisans are found today selling their art from roadside stands along U.S. Highway 17 and in stalls at the Old Market in Charleston's historic district.

Fletcher is best known for his artwork depicting iconic Charleston buildings made of sweetgrass. His work has been featured in Charleston's Piccolo Spoleto Festival.
Handcrafted Palmetto Roses can be purchased from young artisans on busy downtown streets.

OUR SIGNATURE COCKTAIL, "PENINSULA TEA"

What better way to inject art and culture into a cocktail glass! We called our new drink "Peninsula Tea."

Peninsula Tea was so well received in Atlanta that we have served it as our signature cocktail ever since. Our participation in the event exposed us to a new food-and-beverage platform: Festivals, where visitors come from all over the country for a curated culinary experience. Our audience includes the more sophisticated consumer who seeks adventure through food and drink. Since 2015 we have promoted our brand by participating in seminars, demonstrations, cocktail classes and more entertainment events throughout the Southeast.

A Bandit Toast:

To getting by with help from friends

BY TANEKA REAVES

I came to the Holy City in August 2004 as a freshman at the College of Charleston. I was eager and excited to find out what life away from my home in Mullins, S.C. had to offer. I am thankful that it was at the college that I met Johnny Caldwell — my best friend, business partner and fellow Cocktail Bandit.

We both majored in political science, and through my studies I came to realize that there was a huge lack of diversity in Charleston culture, and not just on campus. As Johnny and I checked out local bars and restaurants, we soon realized we often were the only African-American customers. We've never had a problem getting along with others, and the people we met seemed to enjoy our company.

After we finished college, Johnny went to law school while I went looking for a job in politics, which I soon discovered was not easy. I got my first break in 2009 when I was hired as a server in a local saloon. My life changed when I crossed over to the other side of the bar, so to speak. Indeed, the food and beverage industry is a different world. It gave me an opportunity to become an artist in a way I never thought about before. I've long loved a good drink but never thought it would become a career in research and development.

I worked at night in various bars and restaurants in North Charleston and West of the Ashley, where I lived at the time. It was more convenient for me to work close to home, and the income was steady. I also had a day job to get by.

I began crafting and curating my own cocktails at those places, and Johnny and other friends would come in and sample them. I gained confidence with these tastings and soon let other customers sample my custom cocktails. A few of my employers did not like that. Too time consuming and not enough money coming in, they said. They wanted to do things simple and quick, but I wanted to provide their customers with a more enjoyable experience and keep them coming back for more.

I also realized I would not get the best training or opportunities if I stayed put. So, I applied to numerous cocktail-driven bars and restaurants in downtown Charleston. I got no return calls. I consulted with Johnny about the hardships of finding employment in F and B, and she said she was having the same issue with finding employment in the legal field. That's when we decided to work our way into Charleston's social culture through cocktails.

Thus was born the Cocktail Bandits, and it happened at a time when social media started to boom. We studied some business pioneers of social media, like girls who did tutorials on natural hair, make up, exercise — anything that was popular. We were impressed with how they created their brands. We

> **"IT'S BEEN AN INSPIRATIONAL JOURNEY FOR ME BECAUSE OF THE OVERWHELMING SUPPORT OF SO MANY PEOPLE. I LIFT MY GLASS IN A TOAST TO ALL OF YOU. I FEEL FOREVER BLESSED AND THANKFUL!"**
>
> **— Taneka Reaves**

also noted that booze and culture was non-existent online in educational and empowering ways for anyone who looked like us.

We established our website and wrote about cocktails, bartenders, Charleston nightlife — you name it. We described ourselves as "nightlife stylists." We expressed our knowledge and professed our love for the city's party scene from our own perspectives, and lots of people were interested in what we had to say.

The Cocktail Bandits have now arrived! It's been an inspirational journey for me because of the overwhelming support of so many people. I lift my glass in a toast to all of you. I feel forever blessed and thankful!

CHAPTER 3
Port of Rum
Imported slaves, sugar fueled the city's economy

Charleston is a great drinking city, and it has everything to do with being a port. It only takes a sip of life here to feel the spirit. The Holy City's history is long and varied, greatly blessed and terribly tragic — a place that stirs the blood and soothes the soul like a Caribbean rum punch.

By the mid-1600s, the West Indies island of Barbados exported thousands of pounds of sugar primarily to New England, where it was turned into molasses and then into rich, brown rum. From there the rum was shipped to Europe where it sold for cash, much of which went to West Africa where it purchased enslaved men, women and children by the thousands who were hauled like chattel across the Atlantic to what Europeans called the "New World."

It was also from Barbados that the first plantation owners and others moved to Charleston and brought with them enslaved Africans, but sugar did not grow well along the Carolina shore. The landowners turned to growing indigo and rice to make their fortunes.

Many of Charleston's first families were persuaded to settle in Carolina with a promise of cheap, fertile land on which to grow sugar. When that didn't work out, growers experimented with different seeds, including those of rice from Madagascar and other coastal areas of Africa. With the rise of this labor-intensive crop, the settlers aggressively pursued more slave labor specifically for the Africans' stamina and expertise in rice cultivation.

Along with slaves came knowledge of making spicy dark rum. Since the weather did not cooperate with their plans to grow cane on a massive scale, they imported raw sugar from the islands, and thus evolved a small spirits industry based in Charleston.

However, it was enslaved Africans themselves that became one of the Carolina Lowcountry's most valuable commodities, and thus helped establish Charles Town as a hub of economic, culinary and social activities throughout the Southeast. The economic impact nourished by African blood, sweat and tears is obvious in Southern agriculture, trade and customs to this day.

By 1708 the number of black inhabitants of coastal South Carolina surpassed that of whites while rice quickly went from being relatively common grain to a staple in European diets. Meanwhile, it was found that coastal sea island soil could produce incredible crops of long-staple cotton, which was planted, cultivated and harvested by enslaved labor that elevated the planters to become among the richest people in the world.

Today Charleston is a different place. Agriculture has been replaced as the economic engine by tourism and industry.

Liquor, beer and ales

Charleston is known for holding its own

___

The Cocktail Bandits are firm believers in tasty drinks for nearly all occasions. Palomas in summer afternoons are perfection in Charleston, while a Sazerac is an ideal fall nightcap. The list goes on and on.

Indeed, spirits have been popular in the Lowcountry since colonial times. Rum, of course, was first and foremost, while gin came later, so much so that, according to legend, it was blamed for an alcoholism epidemic throughout the Holy City. However, time and peer pressure combined to tamp down bad habits, and most folks around here drink responsibly now.

Today, Charleston has five fine distilleries: Firefly Distillery, High Wire Distilling, Striped Pig Distillery, Charleston Distilling and Red Harbor Rum.

Local spirits have heavily influenced Charleston's social scene and cuisine. In almost every bar or restaurant, you're likely to find some or all of the aforementioned local brands for sipping or mixed in a cocktail. There are not a lot of places in the Southeast that have such a vibrant, diverse and crafted spirits scene.

Firefly Distillery

Firefly Distillery was founded about 30 miles south of Charleston on Wadmalaw Island by Jim Irvin and his wife Ann Limehouse. Scott Newitt joined them more than a decade ago. They lobbied the State Legislature in Columbia, managed to get antiquated

"blue laws" changed and made liquor distillation and production legal again. They named their operation Firefly in honor of the luminous insects that flicker at night throughout the South.

Firefly Distillery created what is known as the world's first Sweet Tea Vodka, distilled from the leaves of the only tea plantation of its kind in South Carolina, The Charleston Tea Plantation, also on Wadmalaw.

In addition to original Sweet Tea Vodka, Firefly distills rum, whiskey and moonshine. We were blessed in February 2017 to sample Firefly's inaugural Bourbon before it hit the market (Coming soon!) and also worked on the production line; we soon decided to leave the hard labor to the pros.

Go online to www.fireflyspirits.com to learn about the distillation process and read about the owners. Sign up for a personalized tour too. You will not be disappointed. You'll also find that they have purchased 16 acres in North Charleston where they plan to open a bigger distillery and expand their retail reach in the fall of 2019.

Striped Pig Distillery

Striped Pig Distillery, off Azalea Drive in North Charleston, holds a special spot in our hearts. It is the first distillery we visited as the Cocktail Bandits. Striped Pig is three years old and produces rum, vodka, moonshine, whiskey and our favorite — gin!

Johnny Pieper, an owner and master distiller, is our favorite person ever! He started in the trade because he saw a need in the Charleston market for homegrown booze. That's when he partnered with a few other gentlemen, built the distillery and named it Striped Pig, also a rum brand prior to Prohibition. Back then, a striped pig's image was painted on a flag outside taverns. Enticed, customers would pay a few coins to see the "striped pig" and would be rewarded with a glass of rum. Today Striped Pig Distillery engages its customers in much the same way and rewards them with an excellent brand of top-notch spirits.

Striped Pig is now a complete grain-to-glass process that sells worldwide. Its corn, rye and wheat seeds come from Myers Farm in Bowman, South Carolina and the mash, fermentation, distillation and bottling is completed in house. You can visit Striped Pig Distillery from 3-7 p.m. on Thursdays and Fridays, and from noon to 5 p.m. on Saturdays. Tell them the Bandits sent you! You can check out their website at www.stripedpigdistillery.com.

Red Harbor Rum

Red Harbor Rum distillery began in 2015 but focuses on Charleston's colonial drinking culture. It is a creation of Justin Buchanan and Jake McDowell. After college, they enrolled in a class at the American Distilling Institute and learned how to make rum. They also worked with other distilleries in the state, including the Striped Pig, and purchased their first still from Six and Twenty distillery in Greenville, South Carolina.

Red Harbor Rum is distilled and rested in new charred barrels, which gives the spirit more of a whiskey or Bourbon cask flavor, as opposed to typical dark rums of today. Justin and Jake found that colonial people did not drink whiskey, so there was no way that the rum could be aged in Bourbon barrels.

The product is made in a small distillery in North Charleston. You can find Red Harbor Rum in several restaurants and bars downtown. We worked with Red Harbor Rum when they first started, and it's great to see the company grow so quickly.

High Wire Distilling Company

High Wire Distilling Company — owned and operated by Scott and Ann Blackwell — is located on upper King Street near the heart of the historic Charleston peninsula. Scott, a "serial entrepreneur," sold his small baking company to General Mills to fulfill his distillery dream. What better place to do so than Charleston!

High Wire makes vodka, rum, revival regular and sorghum Bourbon and our favorite, Hat Trick Gin. High Wire also created an Amaro, a liqueur with Italian influence, that is very interesting for a Southern distillery. High Wire also worked hard to get the liquor laws changed in South Carolina, allowing distilleries to offer tastings and in-house cocktails. This change has opened up job and other opportunities for local bartenders.

Overall, High Wire is a company that is very involved locally, participating in the Charleston Wine and Food Festival and the newly created Bevcon. High Wire also uses homegrown watermelons to make an excellent seasonal brandy.

Charleston Distilling Company

Charleston Distilling, owned by Stephen Heilman opened up in July 2014. Before then, Stephen was living in Illinois with his family and wanted a career change. His dream was to "wear flip flops to work." He had heard stories of his family distilling whiskey during Prohibition and wanted to try his hand at the profession. He did his research and saw that Charleston was an ideal location to create his distillery. After a brief visit, Stephen fell in love with Charleston and moved his family here to open his business.

Charleston Distilling is located in the heart of upper King Street. It is a beautiful independent distillery that produces several craft spirits. They have Jasper's Gin, a whiskey, King Charles Vodka, and our favorite local vodka: Carolina Reaper, made with peppers. Charleston Distilling may be the new distillery on the block, but they have already won several medals for their spirits!

LOCAL SPIRITS ARE HEAVILY INFLUENCED BY OUR CHARLESTON COMMUNITY.

IN ALMOST EVERY BAR OR RESTAURANT, YOU CAN CATCH ONE, TWO, OR EVEN ALL OF THESE LOCAL BRANDS TO BE SIPPED OR MIXED IN A COCKTAIL.

THERE ARE NOT A LOT OF PLACES IN SOUTH CAROLINA, OR IN THE SOUTHEAST IN GENERAL, THAT HAVE SUCH A VIBRANT, DIVERSE AND CRAFTED SPIRITS SCENE.

Holy Beers!

Charleston has a lot of breweries too

The production and sale of handcrafted beer is booming in Charleston. There are 17 breweries in the area now, far more than there were a decade ago; but local brewing is not new around the Holy City, which has a long history of beer consumption.

Beer played a major role in drinking culture of colonial times. Almost everyone drank some type of beer because well water was not treated and cleaned as it is today. "Spruce Beer" — which had low alcoholic content — often graced breakfast tables of the city's earliest homes. It was considered healthier because it killed certain bacteria, yet was low enough in alcohol content to keep imbibers relatively sober.

The first root beer made in Charleston was the "salop," which contained cream. "Shandys" — with citrus juice — emerged with the influx of oranges, lemons and limes from the Caribbean. Fruit juices had short shelf lives so adding beer was a preservative.

Pale ales and dark beers (porters) were abundant back then because they ferment in warmer temperatures. Most were imported from England because it was cheaper, but locals did have success with homebrews.

Edmund Egan was the first Southerner to achieve significant success brewing beer. His was so good that local taverns dropped New England and British brews and served his exclusively for a while. Egan's brewmasters were enslaved Africans — which was not uncommon at that time.

The last major brewery in Charleston before Prohibition was called Germania Brewery. It was formerly the Palmetto Brewery, but the owners thought the name change would be more credible with the city's growing German-immigrant community. However, the United States' entry into World War I seriously flattened sales, and the brewery went bankrupt in 1916.

Prohibition followed and put a stop to legal brewing in the area. This gave rise to Charleston's speakeasy (also known as blind tiger) era. The city was soon known in South Carolina as THE place to purchase and enjoy the best the bootleg industry offered, along with illegal gambling.

Palmetto Brewery

Ed Falkenstein opened Palmetto Brewery in 1993, making it the first public brewery in South Carolina since Prohibition. It was named in honor of the old Palmetto/Germania Brewery that once was downtown at the corner of Hayne and Anson streets. Before Ed opened the new Palmetto Brewery farther up the peninsula on Huger Street, the only craft beers served in the state were Samuel Adams and Sierra Nevada, both of them imports.

Ed did his own research and put up his own money to start the venture. He began with a small tasting room, but state law prohibited it. So, in typical Charleston fashion, he did it anyway, inspiring locals to experiment with various tastes. The company initially brewed pale and amber beers, and as the brand became more popular, Ed got more creative. Today its year-round beers are Palmetto Pale, Amber and Porter as well as Huger Street IPA. They also offer a pilsner and several specialty brews.

Coast Brewing Company

Coast Brewing Company is owned and operated by power couple David Merritt and Jaime Tenny. The brewery opened in 2007 in North Charleston and the story is amazing. David started with a home brewing kit given to him as a birthday gift in 1996. It was supposed to be a gag gift, but he soon proved it otherwise. He later joined the staff in the old Southend Brewery at East Bay and Queen streets before becoming head brewer at Palmetto Brewing.

Eventually he purchased equipment from an out-of-business brewpub and opened Coast Brewing in a building at the old Naval Base in North Charleston. He produced two beers initially — Hop Art and Kolsh — the first organic beers commercially brewed in South Carolina.

Jaime handles all of the paperwork at Coast and is the founder of Pop the Cap S.C. — a grassroots advocacy group committed to lifting the state-mandated alcohol cap of 5 percent to 17.5 percent. Pop the Cap is now called the S.C. Brewers Guild. Helping get the beer laws changed as they did opened the doors to luring other breweries to the state.

Coast Brewing is family friendly and uses only organic ingredients. We love their Kolsh, and are happy Coast has made such a quality imprint on Charleston's beer culture.

Westbrook Brewing

Morgan and Edward Westbrook founded Westbrook Brewing Company in December 2010. Their goal was to provide the Lowcountry with excellent handcrafted beers. Their facility on Ridge Road in Mount Pleasant is state of the art — a large-production business with all of the fixings, including Jack Daniels whiskey barrels and wine barrels. They also experiment with different yeasts that produce a variety of flavors.

Edward was already an accomplished mixologist who knew how to pair great flavors. Two of Westbrook's most popular brews are White Thai and Mexican Cake. Westbrook's goal is to stay on the cutting edge of original customer-tested and flavorful products.

Westbrook is one of the first breweries in Charleston to can its beers in eye-catching green, yellow and white colors. They also have a lot of success with matching their beers with various foods.

Holy City Brewing

Holy City Brewing on Dorchester Road in North Charleston was created in 2011 by four young men, two of whom worked for a rickshaw company, one in biodegradable fuel and one a master brewer. During the slower months of tourism, they decided to home-brew beers. Eventually, they opened Holy City Brewery and it has been a popular hub ever since.

Holy City offers several seasonal beers as well as their staples: Hoppy IPA and a Pluff Mud Porter. The brewery also has a kitchen and the "bar food" is phenomenal (the wings are seasoned with Pluff Mud BBQ sauce). Check out the Holy City Brewing website to set up a tour: www.holycitybrewing.com

Revelry Brewery

Revelry Brewing began as a hobby in a garage by Jay Daratony, Sean Fleming and Ryan Coker. Today their brewery is located at 10 Conroy Street where the focus is on quality craft beer with unusual flavors that include Gullah Cream Ale made from Geechie Boy grits. It is an amazing brew done in the tradition of enslaved African Americans.

Gullah Cream Ale has won several awards, and some of the proceeds from sales support the Gullah-Geechee Corridor Commission, a state-sanctioned organization dedicated to preserving the east coast Gullah and Geechee culture.

Although the name of the award-winning beer raised our eyebrows initially, it is true to the culture and we love it.

Other breweries in and around Charleston include:

Charlestowne Fermentory

Common House Aleworks

Cooper River Brewing

Dockery's Brewing

Edmunds Oast Brewing Co.

Fat Pig Brewing

Fatty's Beer Works

Freehouse Brewing

Frothy Beard Brewing

Ghost Monkey Brewing

LoFi Brewing

Low Tide Brewing

Munkle Brewing

Oak Road Brewing

Pawley's Island Brewing Co.

Rusty Bull Brewing

SNAFU Brewing

Tradesman Brewing

Twisted Cypress

Two Blokes Brewing

Holy Mixers

With a city that is booming with local spirits and local beers, it comes as no surprise that great local mixers are also very popular. Check out the following:

Jack Rudy Cocktail Co.

The Reitz brothers of Leon's Oyster Shop and Little Jack's Tavern are the founders of Jack Rudy Cocktail Co., which is named after their grandfather. This company, based on Market Street in Charleston and in Lexington, Kentucky makes small-batch syrups with an international distribution. Jack Rudy's Elderflower tonic and syrup make the best gin and tonics that we've ever had!

Jack Rudy was an engineer who created a device for pharmacists to count their pills. His grandson Brooks Reitz was inspired by this and designed the tonic syrup bottles to look like medicine bottles from an old-fashioned drug store. We love that!

Bittermilk Mixers /Tippleman's Syrups

With deep roots in the restaurant and bar industry, husband and wife team Joe and MariElena Raya set out to simplify the process of making craft cocktails at home.

Bittermilk is a line of cocktail mixers made for cocktail enthusiasts. Crafted and bottled by human hands in Charleston, the labor is already in the bottle — just add booze.

Each Bittermilk Mixers ingredient includes a sweetener, some acidity and a bitters agent to create a balanced, complex cocktail. The No. 3 Whiskey Sour Mixer and the No. 5 Charred Grapefruit are our favorites. Tonic water can be substituted for alcohol to create mocktails as well.

Tippleman's Handcrafted Syrups are made with cane sugar essential for great flavors in cocktails or mocktails. Some of the most popular syrups are Ginger Honey and Double Spiced Falernum. Yummy!

Cannonborough Beverage Co.

Mike Fendley, Mick Matricciano and Brandon Wogamon are the geniuses who created one of our favorite local sodas — Cannonborough Beverages. Their goal was to take a culinary approach to the world of beverages by making a line of craft sodas that could be used in cocktails or enjoyed with meals.

The crew started about five years ago, serving their sodas at local farmers markets. Now Cannonborough Beverages are wholesaled through local convenience stores and supermarkets. Matricciano and Wogamon are friends since childhood, and worked together at the Gin Joint. They noticed that local spirits and beer were becoming very popular, but there were no local mixers. They developed delicious sodas made with local ingredients, including fresh fruits and herbs from Growfood Carolina, and authentic cane sugar.

Cannonborough beverages come in three flavors: Honey Basil, Grapefruit Elderflower and Ginger Beer, and change seasonally. We have used them in several cocktails served at festivals and they're always a big hit.

O&O Hooch Fizzy Mixer

Jen and Shawn Holland, self-proclaimed "Partners in Lime," are the owners of One and Only Hooch. They have been making this lemon-lime fizzy soda for 15-plus years. It's called Hooch because they started making it for family and friends on the Chattahoochee River before perfecting and marketing it on Sullivan's Island.

This soda is awesome for mixing with all spirits, especially tequila and whiskey. It's now sold in every Walmart store on the Atlantic coast and in all Harris Teeter supermarkets in South Carolina. Their ultimate goal is to be a go-to mixer in bars and restaurants.

One Love Kombucha

In the past few years, we have seen the emergence of a new beverage called Kombucha, a fermented tea consumed for its many health benefits. It helps prevent disease, promotes a healthy gut, is used to help manage diabetes and has many other benefits. Our first time trying this tea was at One Love Kombucha on John's Island.

One Love makes raw, organic, local, Kombucha. The goal is to produce the best beverages while remaining sustainable and seasonal. One Love currently has three amazing flavors: Thai Butterfly, Tumeric Trio and Hibiscus Ginger.

Kombucha is great for cocktails because it has so many nutritional benefits. Restaurants and bars are now making Kombucha cocktails. We are too!

Charleston Tea Plantation

Charleston Tea Plantation is one of a kind. Located on Maybank Highway, Wadmalaw Island, the farm has 127 acres of beautiful tea plants and local wildlife.

Charleston Tea Plantation was purchased by family-owned Bigelow Tea Company in 2003, when it became the dream of Eunice and David Bigelow and local partner Bill Hall to combine talents and share their love of tea as a vibrant piece of Americana for all to enjoy. Today, the plantation is the standard bearer for the long and illustrious American tea story.

Firefly Distillery uses Charleston Plantation Tea in its spirits, as does Jack Rudy Cocktail Co. in its tea syrup. We love making cocktails and mocktails with Charleston Tea, and are delighted it is made practically in our backyard!

Holy Wine

Deep Water Vineyard

Deep Water Vineyard used to be Irving House Vineyards. The new owners, Andrea and Jesse, told us that they always wanted to have a vineyard. When they moved to the South, a few friends saw that the property was for sale and dared them to purchase it from Irving House. So they decided to take that chance, moved their family to Wadmalaw Island, and actually have their own vineyard. They said that it's an exciting, new, overwhelming experience ... sometimes, they feel like they're in "Deep Water" with this new venture.

Deep Water also has a deeper meaning for the co-owners/couple. They feel like the name embodies their view of life: jump in the deep waters and know that you have done something bigger than yourself.

The muscadine grape is the only native grape in the United States and Deep Water is Charleston, South Carolina's only vineyard and winery. They have five muscadine wines that are produced from four grapes. In addition to the Deep Water Muscadine Blend there are two new blends, Driftwood and Sea Island Red, as well as a chardonnay and a cabernet.

Southern Hospitality

Entertaining tips from the Bandit Belles

Charleston welcomes its visitors in grand style. It's a Southern tradition. Many folks who come here for the first time say it's as if they have stepped back in time when they meet the locals and look around.

On any given day in the old city, people dress in historic garb and lead tours of the historic district. You can hear the sounds of horses pulling carriages down the narrow streets and almost taste the Atlantic salt in the air.

Certain unspoken rules of decorum are still practiced in Charleston. It's customary to greet others as you pass along the sidewalks, hold open doors for ladies, and say "yes, sir" or "no ma'am" as terms of respect. It's also important to know that local folks seldom speak ill of the dead or discuss their money, sex and religion.

Long conversations on the street range from the nature of the weather to new grandbabies to how to properly stew a chicken. Sometimes it takes a little prodding when discussing difficult topics. But that's not always the case once you enter the bar scene, where almost any subject is open for debate.

Most local bartenders are easy to talk to, so be careful! You can trust bartender-client confidentiality, but keep it quiet so that others don't hear what you don't want them to know.

After the tragic shooting in the summer of 2015 at Charleston's oldest African-American church — Mother Emanuel AME church, founded in 1816 — the Cocktail Bandits sought a safe place to commiserate with others in mourning. Nine people, including the pastor, were gunned down by a man who was welcomed as a visitor during a Bible study in the basement of the Calhoun Street sanctuary. Soon after the murders, members of the congregation announced that they had forgiven the killer, but not his crimes, and this was critical in keeping a lid on subsequent reactionary street violence. That gesture for non-violence will go down in history as magnanimous.

When the shots were fired, we were in a meeting less than a mile away. It did not take long for word of the tragedy to get around. Grief stricken, we ventured to a neighborhood bar and restaurant packed with people sharing embraces and loving exchanges. Men and women wiped tears from their faces while others openly grieved. We ordered a drink, relieved that we weren't the only ones crying.

People in Charleston are traditional. They hold tightly to their most cherished customs and manners. There's comfort in this, a certain pride in knowing you are a part of something special. Despite one of the most tragic events in Charleston's long history, Southern hospitality is stronger than ever in the Holy City.

Gullah Cuisine

African-American food clears heads, brings people together

You don't have to cure a hangover if you don't have one, but sometimes it does happen. We heard that a combination of aspirin and Vitamin B12 prior to sleep staves off horrible hangover headaches. Others suggest a big pre-party meal, under the assumption that a full stomach blocks the body from absorbing alcohol too quickly.

There is nothing worse than a hangover after a long night out in Charleston, but fear not, there is a Southern solution for those morning-after blues. When you have a hangover, heavy foods — like a pepperoni pizza or greasy cheeseburger and fries — are supposed to work magic. But there are better choices.

In Charleston, food has everything to do with love, and we express it when folks get together for almost anything: receptions, concerts, parties, seminars, you name it. It is customary to deliver dishes to the house when someone moves into the neighborhood or when a baby is born or when a family grieves the loss of a loved one. It's not just the food that comforts us but the sense of community that one feels when sharing a meal and memories with others on just about any occasion.

Chef Benjamin "B.J." Dennis
Photo by Kim Craven

We have a long history of this. Today, chef and scholar Kevin Mitchell of Oxford, Mississippi is committed to educating the culinary community on the monumental impact of the African-American legacy in the evolution of American foods. He cites a man named Nat Fuller who organized a meal for 80 members of the community at the end of the Civil War in 1865, a time when Charleston was most vulnerable.

Chef Mitchell teaches at the University of Mississippi but feels a strong connection to Charleston's dining history. Like many culinary professionals, he was introduced to cooking by the women in his family. His grandmother encouraged him to spend time in the kitchen to observe her techniques. While he watched he developed a love and respect for those who devote their lives to feeding the masses.

On the 150th anniversary of Nat Fuller's original dinner, Mitchell along with fellow food historians, local chefs, restaurant owners and culinary instructors recreated a post-war soiree. McCrady's Tavern in Charleston set the stage for the elaborate meal featuring three types of poultry, turtle soup, pastries, persimmon beer and glasses overflowing with

Chef "BJ" Dennis' Okra Soup

champagne. Some of the proceeds from the dinner have been set aside to fund a Nat Fuller scholarship for students working to pursue careers in the food industry.

Gullah Chef Benjamin "BJ" Dennis has dedicated his career to spreading awareness of Geechee cuisine. Chef Dennis is a Charleston native who represents progressive Southern food culture.

He started as a dishwasher in busy restaurants downtown while attending classes in Trident Tech-nical College's popular culinary-studies program. Chef BJ has since traveled extensively throughout the American South and the Caribbean learning oral traditions from elders and experimenting with rare African grains and incredibly hard to find beans. He encourages others to consider a more plant- and whole-grain-based diet along with lots of fresh sea-food. He credits such a diet for the continued health and longevity of people in Barbados whose dishes were originally prepared by enslaved plantation workers.

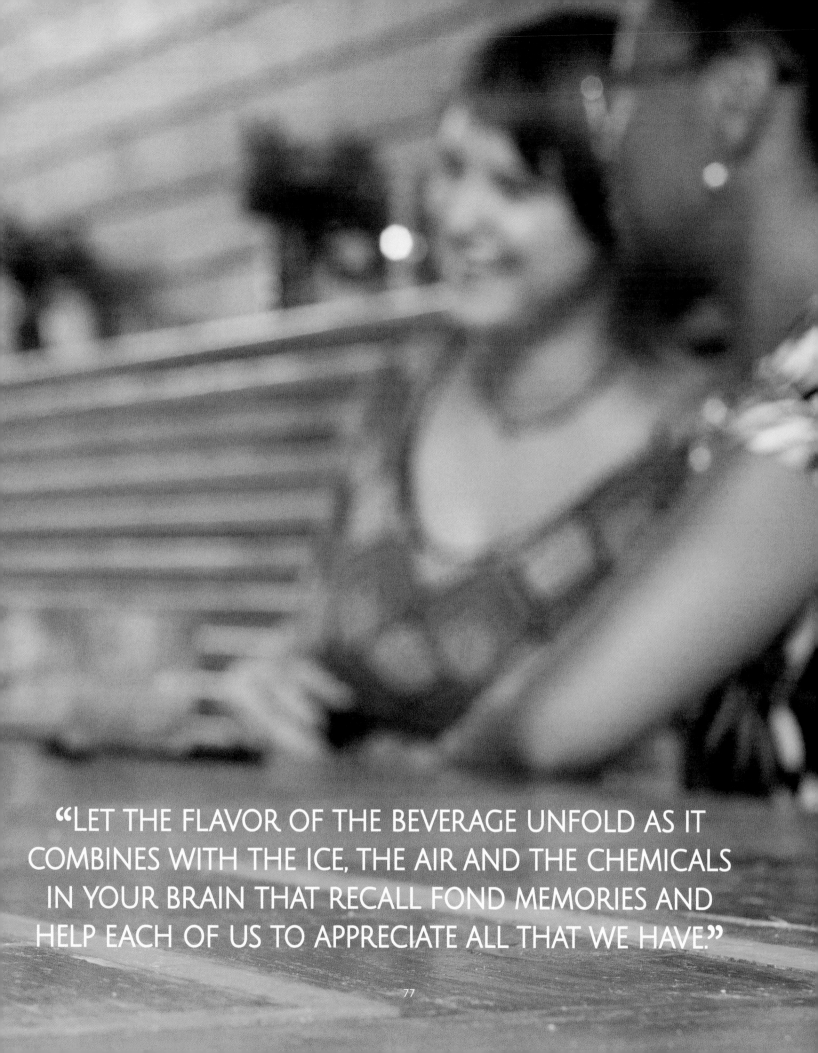

"LET THE FLAVOR OF THE BEVERAGE UNFOLD AS IT COMBINES WITH THE ICE, THE AIR AND THE CHEMICALS IN YOUR BRAIN THAT RECALL FOND MEMORIES AND HELP EACH OF US TO APPRECIATE ALL THAT WE HAVE."

In Closing ...

We all must drink something. Right? Most doctors recommend lots of water daily, but there's much more to be said about whetting one's whistle in Cocktail Bandits fashion.

Our goal is to elevate the way you think about what you drink, whether you enjoy beverages shaken, blended or stirred. There is indeed a cocktail for every occasion to quench thirsts while enjoying life along with friends and family. We believe that alcohol is not harmful when consumed responsibly.

A glass of red wine a day helps ward off heart disease, as does a careful blend of fruit and vegetables and spirits. Fermented liquids are often nature's medicine and should be respected as such. As with all things, moderation is the key. So, take your time making every cocktail because crafting is part of the experience. Savor each sip. Let the flavor of the beverage unfold as it combines with the ice, the air and the chemicals in your brain that recall fond memories and help each of us to appreciate all that we have.

Over indulgence spoils the process. It's as easy as dialing 9-1-1, and always remember to never drink and drive.

CHAPTER 4

Holy Spirits! Recipes

Pushing the limits of our friendship even further, we asked for crafted cocktail recipes from each mixologist. Every sip is intended to invoke the essence of Charleston.

Evan Christy demonstrates a proper pour.

ABOUT THE RECIPES

CRAFTING COCKTAILS ARE ALL ABOUT ACCURACY.
WHEN USING EXOTIC AND SOMETIMES
FUNKY INGREDIENTS LIKE BALSAMIC VINEGAR,
MEASUREMENTS BECOME INCREASINGLY
IMPORTANT. TOO MUCH OF ANYTHING CAN RUIN
A GOOD THING.

WE OPTED TO USE MILLILITERS WHEN LISTING THE
LIQUID AMOUNT. THIS ALLOWS FOR CONTROLLED
INCORPORATION IN THE COCKTAIL, CREATING
A MORE BALANCED AND ENJOYABLE DRINKING
EXPERIENCE. FOR YOUR QUICK REFERENCE, 15ML IS
ROUGHLY ½ OUNCE.

PENINSULA TEA

Ingredients:

- 60 ml Firefly Sweet Tea Vodka
- 25 ml Fresh Lemon Juice
- 25 ml Tippleman's Ginger Honey Syrup
- Topped with Blenheim Spicy Ginger Ale
- Garnish: Lemon wheel, mint sprig and handcrafted palmetto rose

What to do:

Add sweet tea vodka, syrup and lemon juice to mixing tin. Shake vigorously. Fill mason jar with ice; add mixture. Top with ginger soda. Lovingly place lemon wheel on the edge of the jar. Place mint in the palm of your hand; Smack your hands together passionately releasing mint oils and aroma. Place mint in jar. Add handmade palmetto rose. Sip through a straw.

Imagine sipping the Peninsula Tea on your porch at sunset. Southern perfection!

AFRO ALCHEMY

Ingredients:

- 670 ml Vodka
- 30 ml Blue Curaçao
- 30 ml Fresh Lemon juice
- Tonic Water
- Garnish: Edible Gold Flakes

What to do:

Add vodka, blue curacao and lemon juice to mixing tin; partially fill with ice and shake. Fill rocks glass with ice. Pour in cocktail mixture. Top with tonic water. Sprinkle gold flakes. Enjoy.

BARNFLY

Ingredients:

- 60 ml Cathead Vodka
- 40 ml Fresh Lemon Juice
- 30 ml Basil & Sage Syrup
- Hooch Fizzy Mixer
- Garnish: Basil leaf, Lemon Wheel

What to do:

Add vodka, lemon juice and syrup to mixing tin full of ice. Shake purposefully. Strain over ice in chilled glass. Top with Hooch. Place garnish. Enjoy.

FRESH BLUSH

Ingredients:

- 60 ml Cathead Vodka
- 25 ml Fresh Lime Juice
- 50 ml Fresh Pineapple Juice
- 25 ml Grenadine
- Topped Tonic Water

What to do:

Add vodka, lime juice, pineapple juice and grenadine to mixing tin; fill with ice. Shake passionately. Add ice to clean pint glass. Strain cocktail mixture over ice. Gently top cocktail with tonic water. Lovingly place pineapple leaf and lime wheel garnish. Sip slowly with straw.

A delicate blend of Vodka and fresh juice. Perfect for afternoon sips.

FIRE FLYING ON THE ISLAND

Ingredients:

- 60 ml Firefly Sweet Tea Vodka
- 20 ml Brown Sugar Syrup
- 30 ml Pineapple Juice
- 15 ml Lemon Juice
- Prosecco
- Lemon Wheel Garnish

What to do:

Add Firefly vodka, syrup, pineapple and lemon juice into a mixing tin. Add ice and shake. Pour into tall rocks glass. Top with prosecco. Garnish with lemon wheel.

THE BLONDE REAPER

Ingredients:

- 45 ml Carolina Reaper Vodka
- 20 ml Carrot Juice
- 15 ml Local Spiced Honey
- 60 ml Natural Blonde Bloody Mary Mix
- Parsley and Shredded Carrot Garnish

What to do:

Pour Reaper Vodka, carrot juice and honey into a mixing tin. Shake. Pour contents into a large glass and top with Natural Blonde Bloody Mary Mix. Garnish with parsley and shredded carrots.

GRAPEFRUIT BLISS

Ingredients:

- 60 ml High Wire Vodka
- 15 ml Freshly Squeezed Grapefruit Juice
- Cannonborough Grapefruit Elderflower Soda
- Agave Syrup
- Garnish: Rosemary Sprig; Grapefruit Slice

What to do:

Muddle grapefruit slices (no skin) into mixing tin with grapefruit juice and agave syrup. Add vodka, ice, and shake. Pour contents in Collins glass. Top with Cannonborough Grapefruit Elderflower soda. Garnish with grapefruit slice (with skin) and a rosemary sprig.

HIBISCUS CHUCKTOWN MULE

Ingredients:

- 60 ml Charleston Distilling Vodka
- 15 ml Lemon Juice
- 15 ml Hibiscus Syrup
- Cannonborough Ginger Beer
- Garnish: Hibiscus Flower

What to do:

Pour vodka, hibiscus syrup and lemon juice in a mixing tin. Shake. Pour contents and Cannonborough Ginger Beer into an iced copper cup. Garnish with hibiscus flower. Serve!

PHOENIX

Ingredients:

- 60 ml Blanco Tequila
- 25 ml Agave Syrup
- 40 ml Fresh Grapefruit Juice
- 50 ml Pomegranate Juice
- Garnish: Grapefruit Slice

What to do:

In a mixing tin, add tequila, agave syrup, lime juice and pomegranate juice. Add ice to tin and shake. Pour mixture into rocks glass. Place grapefruit garnish. Sip.

Fox Trap

Ingredients:

- 50 ml Blanco Tequila
- 50 ml Cucumber Water
- 25 ml Fresh Lime Juice
- 35 ml Jack Rudy Elderflower Syrup
- Topped with Tonic Water
- Garnish: Hibiscus Salt Ice Block

What to do:

Add tequila, cucumber water, lime juice and elderflower syrup to mixing tin; fill with ice. Shake passionately. Strain mixture into chilled rocks glass. Delicately place hibiscus salt ice block. Drink responsibly.

This color-changing cocktail impresses every sipper!

BLACKER THE BERRY

Ingredients:

- 60 ml Tequila
- 30 ml Local Blackberry Purée
- Topped with O and O Limeade Hooch
- Jamaican Bitters
- Garnish with Sage L eaf

What to do:

Boil ½ cup blackberries down with equal parts water and sugar to create purée. After it has cooled, pour purée and tequila into mixing glass with ice. Shake. Pour contents into iced glass. Top with Hooch. Add 2 dashes of Jamaican bitters. Garnish with blackberries and a sage leaf.

PORGY & BESS

Ingredients:

- 560 ml Watermelon Water
- 25 ml Fresh Lime Juice
- 50 ml Reposado Tequila
- 25 ml Agave Syrup
- Semi-Sweet Cider

What to do:

Add watermelon water, lime juice, agave and tequila to mixing tin. Fill mixing tin with ice. Shake deliberately. Fill a Collins glass with ice. Strain cocktail mixture over ice. Pour cider into glass. Take gentle lady sips.

Such ciders are making a serious splash in the beverage market. Apples vary in taste ranging from super sweet to mouth-puckering tart. Cideries are producing an assortment of flavors to act as an affordable alternative for champagne or prosecco.

This cocktail was inspired by the Southern folk opera, "Porgy & Bess," written by Charlestonian DuBose Heyward.

BANDITA AMOR

Ingredients:
- 45 ml Reposado Tequila
- 20 ml High Wire Amaro
- 10 ml Agave Syrup
- 30 ml Grapefruit Juice
- Club Soda (optional)
- Garnish: Grapefruit Slice

What to do:
Pour all contents into an iced mixing tin. Strain into a cocktail glass or coupe glass. Top with club soda (optional). Garnish with grapefruit slice.

CHUCKTOWN FROZEN STRAWBERRY MARGARITA

Ingredients:
- 60 ml Tequila
- 20 ml Fresh Orange Juice
- 15 ml Lime Juice
- 30 ml Local Honey Syrup
- Garnish: Fresh Strawberries

What to do:
Place all ingredients into blender. Add ice. Blend. Pour blended beverage in margarita glass. Garnish with strawberries.

FAMILY PORTRAIT

Ingredients:
- 60 ml Anejo Tequila
- 30 ml Sherry
- 30 ml Cherry Syrup
- 20 ml Fresh Grapefruit Juice
- Garnish: Cherry

What to do:
Add Tequila, cherry syrup and grapefruit juice to mixing tin. Shake passionately. Add ice to clean glass. Strain cocktail mixture over ice. Add sherry float. Garnish with cherry on top.

PORT OF COUPES

Ingredients:
- 50 ml Anejo Tequila
- 25 ml Toasted Bitter Oak Syrup
- 25 ml Fresh Lime Juice
- Topped with Hooch Limeade Soda
- Garnish: Mint and Lime Wheel

What to do:
In mixing tin full of ice, add tequila, oak syrup, lime juice. Secure shaker lid then shake passionately. Pour mixture into glass full of ice. Top with Hooch. Garnish with mint and lime wheel. Stir and sip with straw for best taste.

DILL - WITH IT

Ingredients:

- 45 ml Tequila
- 15 ml Lime Juice
- Cucumber
- 10 ml Dill Syrup
- Jack Rudy Tonic
- Garnish: Dill Sprig

What to do:

Muddle 1 slice of cucumber in bottom of shaker. Add tequila, lime juice, dill syrup and ice. Shake. Pour contents in an iced glass. Top with Jack Rudy Tonic and garnish with dill sprig.

LA BANDITA LAGERITA

Ingredients:

- 45 ml Jalapeño infused (optional) tequila
- 20 ml Fresh squeezed lemon and lime juice
- 20 ml Cointreau
- Lo-Fi Mexican Lager
- Garnish: Lime Salt Rim, Jalapeno slice

What to do:

Pour jalapeño-infused (optional) tequila, freshly squeezed lemon and lime juice, and Cointreau into a mixing glass. Shake vigorously. Rim highball glass with lime juice and dip the rim into the salt. Add ice. Pour all contents into iced highball glass. Top with Lo-Fi Mexican Lager. Garnish with jalapeño slice.

This Cocktail Bandit Original Cocktail can be found locally at all SOL Southwest locations!

SKYWALKER

Ingredients:

- 50 ml of Spiced Rum
- 40 ml of Pineapple Juice
- 30 ml of Fresh Lime Juice
- 30 ml of Fresh Lemon Juice
- 40 ml of Pomegranate Juice
- 40 ml of Cointreau (or other Orange Liqueur)
- Garnish: Pineapple Wedge or Pomegranate Seeds

What to do:

Fill a cocktail shaker with ice and pour in rum, Cointreau and fruit juices. Place lid and shake vigorously. Fill tall glass with ice. Strain cocktail mixture over ice. Place garnish. Enjoy.

"Skywalker" is great in a punch bowl for entertaining guests!

BLACK GIRL MAGIC

Ingredients:
- 60 ml Afro Head Dark Rum
- ¼ Cup of Blackberries
- 30 ml Fresh Lime Juice
- Tonic Water
- Dried Fruit Bitters
- Garnish: Blackberries and Lime Peel

What to do:
Add blackberries to mixing glass. Smash blackberries with muddler. Pour rum and lime juice into mixing glass. Add ice and secure shaker lid. Shake passionately. Fill rocks glass with ice. Strain contents of mixer into rocks glass. Top with tonic. Delicately add 3 drops of vanilla bitters. Place vanilla bean garnish. Take #GentleLadySips.

RUM DAY CAP

Ingredients:
- 30 ml Striped Pig Spiced Rum
- 30 ml Kahlua
- 15ml Coconut Milk
- Cola

What to do:
Place spiced rum, Kahlua and coconut milk into an iced tin. Shake. Pour into iced rocks glass and top with cola.

SPICE AND EVERYTHING NICE

Ingredients:

- 30 ml Striped Pig Spiced Rum
- 15 ml Orange Liqueur
- 15 ml Lime Juice
- 15 ml Passion Fruit Purée
- Garnish: Citrus slices, Mint

What to do:

Pour all ingredients into mixing tin. Shake.
Pour all contents into an iced rocks glass. Garnish with citrus slices and mint.

ONE IN A MELON

Ingredients:
- 45 ml Red Harbor Rum
- 20 ml Melon Liqueur
- 15 ml Pineapple Juice
- 15 ml Lime juice
- O and O Hooch Limeade Soda
- Garnish: Pineapple Slice and Leaf

What to do:
Mix rum, melon liqueur, pineapple juice and lime juice into mixing tin with ice. Shake. Pour into iced Collins glass. Topped with O and O Hooch. Garnish with pineapple slice and leaf.

Amazing in a punch bowl!

THUNDER GARDEN

Ingredients:

- 50 ml of Flor de Cana White Rum
- 25 ml Muscadine Syrup
- 1 Bar Spoon of Cucumber Syrup
- 25 ml Fresh Lemon Juice
- Topped with Cannonborough Grapefruit Elderflower Soda
- Garnished with Muscadine & Cucumber Ice Block

What to do:

Add rum, lemon juice, muscadine syrup and cucumber syrup to mixing tin. Add ice. Shake passionately. In a rocks glass, place cucumber ice block. Pour mixture over ice. Top with Elderflower Soda. Slice grape to the center then place on the rim of the glass. Enjoy!

Muscadine grapes are native to the Carolinas and are often used for home wine making.

CABIN FEVER

Ingredients:

- 60 ml of Gin
- 60 ml Unsweetened Hibiscus Tea
- 20 ml of Spicy Cinnamon Syrup
- 25 ml Fresh Lemon Juice
- 30 ml Pineapple Juice

What to do:

Add gin, hibiscus tea and syrup to mixing tin. Shake passionately. Fill glass with ice. Add lemon and pineapple juice. Pour contents into glass. Lovingly place garnishes. Imbibe.

GLASS DOOR

Ingredients:

- 25 ml Cassis Liqueur
- 60 ml Bristow Gin
- 25 ml Fresh Lime Juice
- 50 ml Pineapple Juice
- Topped with Cannonborough Ginger Beer
- Garnish: Lavender Ice Cube

What to do:

In a mixing tin full of ice, add gin, juice and Cassis. Shake purposefully. Strain mixture into chilled rocks glass. Pour in ginger beer. Lovingly place lavender ice cube. Sip through straw. Enjoy.

Gentle Lady Gimlet

Ingredients:

- 60 ml Bristow Gin
- 25 ml Fresh Lime Juice
- 25 ml Alley Tonic Syrup
- Topped with Tonic Water
- Garnished with Cucumber Slices

What to do:

Fill a cocktail shaker with ice and pour in gin, juice and syrup. Place lid and shake vigorously. Fill tall glass with ice. Strain cocktail mixture over ice. Top with tonic water. Take Gentle Lady Sips.

Our twist on a classic gin and tonic.

PARTY LINE

Ingredients:

- 60 ml of Bristow Gin
- 60 ml Oliver Pluff Hibiscus Tea
- 20 ml of Honey
- 25 ml Fresh Lime Juice
- Garnish: Lime Twist

What to do:

Add gin, lime juice, tea and honey to mixing tin. Shake passionately. Pour contents into martini glass. Lovingly sprinkle dried tea garnish and place lime twist on the rim of the glass. Enjoy.

GIN

CHARLESTON SINGLE

Ingredients:

- 60 ml Gin
- 25 ml Fresh Grapefruit Juice
- 20 ml Cucumber Syrup
- Tonic Water
- Garnish: Cucumber slices

What to do:

Cut cucumber into cubes. Place into mixing tin. Use muddler to smash cucumber releasing the liquid. Add gin, lemon juice, syrup and ice. Shake passionately. Strain into highball glass.

POWERSUIT

Ingredients:

- 25 ml Fresh Lemon Juice
- 30 ml Gin
- Topped with Prosecco (or other sweet champagne)

What to do:

Add gin and juice to mixing tin. Shake passionately. Pour into chilled fluted coupe. Top with Prosecco. #GentleLadySips.

Pour this up and let the magic happen!

THE BLUE BULLY

Ingredients:

- Blueberries
- 45 ml Jasper Gin
- 15 ml Lemon juice
- 15 ml Simple syrup
- Red Bull Blueberry Energy Beverage
- Garnish: blueberries; rosemary

What to do:

Muddle blueberries with simple syrup and lemon juice in mixing tin. Add gin and ice. Shake. Pour items in iced Collins glass. Top with Red Bull Blueberry Energy Beverage. Garnish with blueberry and rosemary.

FLOWER CROWN

Ingredients:

- 60 ml Striped Pig Gin
- 15 ml Jack Rudy Elderflower Tonic
- Topped with Grapefruit Elderflower Soda
- Garnish: Edible Flowers

What to do:

Pour gin and elderflower tonic into iced mixing tin. Shake. Pour in iced rocks glass and top with Cannonborough Grapefruit Elderflower Soda. Garnish with edible flowers.

LADY IN RED

Ingredients:

- 60 ml Striped Pig Gin
- 15 ml Rosemary Simple Syrup
- 1 Blood Orange
- Garnish: Rosemary, Blood Orange Slice

What to do:

Pour gin, rosemary simple syrup and the juice from 1 blood orange into an iced shaker. Shake vigorously. Strain into an iced glass. Garnish with blood orange slice and rosemary sprig.

LIVING LA VIDA LOCAL

Ingredients:

- 45 ml Hat Trick Gin
- 15 ml Jack Rudy Tonic
- 15 ml Pineapple juice
- 10 ml Lime Juice
- Topped with Ginger Beer
- Garnish Lime Wedge; Thyme

What to do:

Pour all contents (except ginger beer) into mixing tin. Shake. Pour all ingredients into a low rocks glass. Add ginger beer. Garnish with lime wedge and sprig of thyme.

Marianne Rogers

Upstate Revival

Ingredients:

- 60 ml Six & Twenty 5-Grain Bourbon
- 20 ml Fresh Lime Juice
- 40 ml Peach Juice
- 25 ml Bittermilk Charred Grapefruit Tonic
- O & O Hooch Limeade
- Garnish: Basil Leaf, Freshly Sliced Peaches

What to do:

Add Bourbon, lime juice, peach juice and grapefruit tonic to mixing tin full of ice. Shake passionately. Pour into rocks glass full of ice. Add Hooch soda. Garnish with basil leaf and peach slice. Sip.

THE GINGER LADY

Ingredients:

- 45 ml Virgil Kaine Ginger Bourbon Whiskey
- 15 ml Tippleman's Ginger Honey syrup
- 15 ml Lime Juice
- Topped with Cannonborough Honey Basil Soda
- Garnish Lime Wheel and Basil Leaf

What to do:

Pour all the contents into an iced mixing tin. Shake. Pour cocktail into an iced rock glass. Top with Honey Ginger Soda. Garnish with basil leaf.

NEW CHARLESTON SOUR

Ingredients:

- 45 ml Revival Sorghum Bourbon Whiskey
- 20 ml Bittermilk Charred Grapefruit Tonic
- Topped with Soda water
- Garnish: Grapefruit Slice; Mint

What to do:

Pour Sorghum Bourbon Whiskey and Charred Grapefruit Tonic into mixing tin. Shake. Pour into iced rocks glass. Top with soda water. Garnish with grapefruit slice and mint.

PAMA PARADISE

Ingredients:

- 15ml PAMA Pomegranate Liqueur
- 30ml Virgil Kaine Bourbon Whiskey
- Topped with O and O Hooch Lemon Lime Soda
- Garnish: Lime Wedge; Pomegranate Seeds

What to do:

Pour PAMA and Bourbon into iced rocks glass. Stir contents with bar spoon. Top with lemon lime soda. Garnish with pomegranate seeds and lime wedge. Serve.

LOWCOUNTRY SUNSETS

Ingredients:

- 60 ml Sorghum Bourbon Whiskey
- 30 ml Jack Rudy's Tonic
- Topped with One Love Turmeric Kombucha
- Garnish Lime Wedge
- Turmeric Powder

What to do:

Pour Sorghum Bourbon Whiskey and tonic into a mixing tin. Add ice. Shake. Pour contents in rocks glass with ice or pour straight up in rocks glass. Top with One Love Tumeric Trio Kombucha. Dip lime wedge in turmeric powder or garnish on side of your glass. Serve.

CAROLINA SHANDY

Ingredients:

- 1 part Cannonborough Honey Basil Soda
- 1 part Pabst Blue Ribbon

What to do:

Fill chilled pint glass halfway with PBR then top with Cannonborough Honey Basil Soda. Sprinkle hops on top as garnish.

Charleston is home to a bar that sells more cans of Pabst Blue Ribbon than any other bar in the world! Located on Upper King Street, the Recovery Room is every food and beverage professional's late-night spot. Regulars order a $1.25 PBR and a shot of Jameson. Turn up! Our shandy is a great way to enjoy craft soda and cheap, good beer.

Morning Glory

Ingredients:

- 60 ml Strawberry Puree
- 40 ml Lemon Juice
- 40 ml Lime Juice
- Brut Champagne
- Garnish: Strawberry Leaf

What to do:

Add strawberries and fruit juice to chilled champagne glass. Carefully top with champagne. Imbibe.

THE LEGENDARY PORTER

Ingredients:

- 30 ml High Wire Amaro
- 30 ml Orange Juice
- Topped with Holy City Pluff Mud Porter
- Garnish: Orange Wheel

What to do:

Pour Amaro and orange juice into mixing tin with ice. Shake. Strain contents into beer mug and topped with Holy City Pluff Mud Porter. Garnish with orange wheel.

MAGNOLIA SONG

Ingredients:
- 25 ml Fresh Lemon Juice
- 15 ml Agave Syrup
- 30 ml Shrub
- Topped with Hooch
- Garnish: Cucumber Slice, Flower Petal

What to do:
In a glass full of ice, add shrub and lemon juice. Slowly add Hooch. Stir with straw for best taste. Enjoy.

VIRGIN GRAPEFRUIT SOUR

Ingredients:
- 60 ml Bittermilk Charred Grapefruit Tonic
- Topped with Soda Water
- Garnish: Grapefruit Wedge

What to do:
Pour Charred Grapefruit Tonic into a small iced, rocks glass. Top with soda water. Garnish. Serve.

Blue Whale

Ingredients:

- 50 ml Blue Hibiscus Tea
- 25 ml Rosemary Syrup
- 30 ml Fresh Lime Juice

What to do:

In glass mixing jar, combine blue tea, syrup and lime juice. Gently stir with bar spoon. Strain into tall glass full of ice. Enjoy with straw.

GRANDMA'S SWEET TEA

Ingredients:

- 60 ml Unsweetened Freshly Brewed Tea
- 1 bar spoon of Local Honey
- 1 bar spoon of Brown Sugar
- 40 ml Pineapple Juice
- 20 ml Lemon Juice
- Garnish: Pineapple Leaf, Lime Peel

What to do:

In glass mixing jar, combine tea, honey, brown sugar, pineapple and lemon juice. Gently stir with bar spoon. Strain into tall glass full of ice. Place lemon garnish. Sip.

Use the natural sweetness from fruit juice to reduce sugar usage. Not your typical sweet tea but just as refreshing.

A PLACE IN THYME

Crafted by Jeremiah Schenzel of South Seas Tiki Lounge

Ingredients:

- 70 ml 3-year-old Rum
- 40 ml Madeira
- 30 ml ChiCha (Peruvian purple corn syrup)
- 50 ml Pineapple Juice
- Garnish: Brulee Pineapple

What to do:

Add rum, pineapple juice and ChiCha to mixing tin full of ice. Shake. Fill rocks glass with ice. Strain cocktail mixture over ice. Place pineapple garnish. Enjoy.

Schenzel was inspired by Charleston's many Afro-Caribbean influences when he created a syrup from ChiCha, a Peruvian purple corn. This ingredient adds a spicy and mild earthy element to every sip. His use of Madeira pays homage to the classic fortified wine that was all the rave in the 18th century. For us, Jeremiah crafted a cocktail that was vibrant, while respecting tradition. He mixed three-year-old rum, homemade corn syrup, pineapple juice and Madeira. "A Place in Thyme" is playfully fortified and reflects Charleston's diverse history.

AGAINST THE GRAIN

Crafted by Allen Lancaster of The Spectator Hotel

Ingredients:

- 60 ml Highwire New Southern 4 Grains Bourbon
- 30 ml Liquore Strega
- 25 ml Sake
- 50 ml Butternut Squash Puree
- 2 dashes Fee Brothers Orange Bitters
- Garnish: Orange Twist/Red Bell Pepper

What to do:

In a mixing tin, add Bourbon, Strega, sake puree and bitters. Drop in a few cubes of ice, then shake for at least 10 seconds. Fill rocks glass with ice. Strain mixture into glass. Place pepper and orange garnish. Drink responsibly.

Lancaster is largely influenced by his travels, which is clearly reflected in his creations. His "Against The Grain" cocktail combines sake, blended Bourbon and butternut squash puree. This drink smells like an autumn harvest with a velvety mouthfeel.

FREEDOM OF PEACH

Crafted by Megan Deschaine of The Macintosh

Ingredients:

- 60 ml Belle Meade Madeira Cask Finish Bourbon
- 50 ml Freshly Brewed Black Tea
- 40 ml Homemade Peach Cordial
- 30 ml Fresh Lemon Juice
- 30 ml Honey Syrup
- ½ cup of Peach Slices (to muddle and garnish)

What to do:

In mixing glass, muddle fresh peaches. Add all Bourbon, peach cordial, black tea, honey syrup and lemon juice to a shaking tin. Shake well with ice. Fill rocks glass with ice. Strain mixture into glass. Garnish with peach slice. Enjoy.

This fruit-forward cocktail features local peaches and cask-aged Madeira. The addition of muddled fruit provides this cocktail with much needed texture and creaminess. Did you know that South Carolina is the second largest producer of peaches behind California, not Georgia? "Freedom of Peach" is perfect for summer sipping.

Photos by Tyler's Eye

QUEEN OF KINGS

Crafted by Rochelle Jones of Stars Restaurant Rooftop & Grill Room

Ingredients:

- 60 ml Virgil Kaine Rye Whiskey
- 40 ml Cardamaro Amaro
- 40 ml Luxardo Liqueur
- 60 ml Southern Twist Bison Grass Cocktail Infusion
- 2 dashes of Angostura Bitters
- 2 dashes of Creole Bitters
- Garnish: Brandied Cherries and Orange Twist

What to do:

In a mixing tin, add whiskey, amaro, Luxardo, Bison Grass Infusion and bitters. Add in a few cubes of ice, then shake for at least 10 seconds. Fill rocks glass with ice. Strain mixture into glass. Garnish with cherries and orange twist. Cheers.

Cocoa Rae

MEXICAN COMPROMISE

Crafted by Ramon Caraballo of The Rarebit

Ingredients:
- 60 ml Blanco Tequila
- 40 ml Cointreau
- 40 ml Amaro
- Garnish: Ice Block and Orange Peel

What to do:
Fill mixing glass with ice. Add all ingredients. Stir mixture gently with bar spoon. Strain mixture into chilled rocks glass. Gently place ice block in rocks glass. Rub fresh orange peel around the rim of the glass. Place peel over ice block. Enjoy.

Cocoa Rae

Ramon created a booze-forward tequila cocktail to reflect the rise in consumer awareness of the Mexican spirit.

165

ABOUT THE COCKTAIL BANDITS

Johnny Caldwell and Taneka Reaves, named two of Charleston's 50 Most Progressive in 2016 and listed among Imbibe Magazine's "75 People to Watch in 2018," are the dynamic duo known around the globe as the curly-haired Cocktail Bandits. These full-time Charleston Beverage Ambassadors met at the College of Charleston, and now, with their booming hospitality business and self-titled Cocktail Bandits blog, promote female empowerment through advocacy for the food and beverage community from a feminine, urban perspective.

The curly ladies, who talk cocktails daily, educate and entertain their growing blog audience through their own original cocktail recipes, by promoting the craftsmanship of other bar professionals and by sharing their experiences at foodie events all around the Holy City and beyond. Johnny and Taneka have hosted sold-out events at Charleston Food & Wine Festival, Atlanta Food & Wine Festival and Euphoria Greenville Food, Wine & Music Festival. As expert judges, the Cocktail Bandits have participated in the American Craft Spirit Competition, First Annual Fried Chicken Challenge, Charleston Fashion Week's Top Cocktail Competition and more!

The duo have also been featured on Sirius XM Radio online, NBC BLK online, Metro UK online, Style Me Pretty Online, Cuisine Noir Magazine, Black Southern Belle Magazine, National PBS TV's "Moveable Feast with Fine Cooking", ESSENCE Magazine and several other regional publications. The Bandits have collaborated with brands Red Bull, Avion Tequila, Saveur Magazine, Renaissance Hotel and Toyota to transform the way people think about beverages.

REFERENCES

Agave Syrup

1 part Agave
1 part Distilled Water

Combine water and agave in bottle. Shake mixture. Store until use. Agave syrup mixes better in cocktail than thick, raw agave.

Basil + Sage Syrup

Add 3 cups of water to medium pot. Place on stove and let boil. Delicately place basil and sage leaves into water. Add 1.5 cups of white sugar. Stir until sugar dissolves. Let steep. Remove from heat. After allowing syrup to cool, pour into jar. Store in the refrigerator until use.

Blue Hibiscus Tea

In tea kettle, bring water to boil. Add hibiscus tea; let steep. Allow tea to cool before use in cocktail. Store in refrigerator.

Brulee Pineapple

Remove stem from ripe pineapple. Slice pineapple on its side; this will leave you with whole circles of pineapple. Cut into triangle by slicing an "X" shape. Gently sprinkle sugar over pineapple wedge. In secure area, use torch to warm sugar until brown. Let caramelized pineapple cool before use.

Butternut Squash Puree

Butternut Squash
Red Chili Peppers
Saffron
Apple Cider Vinegar
Maple Syrup

Halve the squash lengthwise and remove the seeds and strings. Place on a roasting pan, skin side down. Bake in a preheated 350-degree oven for 30 to 40 minutes or until fork tender. Remove the squash from the oven, scoop out the flesh and place in a food processor. Add the red chilli peppers, saffron, apple cider vinegar and maple syrup. Puree until smooth. Pulse a few times to incorporate. Bottle and refrigerate until use.

Cucumber Ice

Shave the skin from ripe cucumber. Fill block ice mold with cucumber shaving. Place in freezer to harden. Store in freezer until use.

Cucumber Syrup

Add 3 cups of water to medium pot. Add 1.5 cups of white sugar. Stir until sugar dissolves. Place on stove and bring to medium heat. Peel and slice a ripe cucumber. Add slice to pot and cook for 3 minutes. Remove from heat. After allowing syrup to cool, strain into clean jar. Store in the refrigerator.

Cucumber Water

Peel the skin from ripe cucumber. Use vegetable juice to extract liquid from cucumber. Strain into clean bottle. Refrigerate until use.

Hibiscus Salt Ice Block

In clean ice mold, fill with water leaving room at the top. (This gives the ice room to expand as it freezes). Sprinkle hibiscus salt over water. Place mold in freezer; let harden. Remove from mold. Store in freezer until use.

Hibiscus Tea

In tea kettle, bring water to boil. Add hibiscus tea; let steep. Allow tea to cool before use in cocktail. Store in refrigerator.

Hibiscus Tea Ice Cube

In clean ice mold, add room temperature hibiscus tea leaving room at the top. (This gives the ice room to expand as it freezes). Place mold in freezer; let harden. Remove from mold. Store in freezer until use.

Honey Syrup

1 part honey
1 part water

Combine water and honey in bottle. Shake mixture. Store until use. Honey syrup mixes better in cocktail than thick, raw honey.

Lavender Ice Cube

Fill clean ice mold with water. Leave space at the top for the ice to expand. Sprinkle lavender pieces on top of the water. Place mold in freezer; let harden. Remove from mold. Store in freezer until use.

When placing lavender cube in cocktail, avoid wetting the top of the ice cube. This keeps the lavender pieces in place.

Muscadine Syrup

2 cups of muscadine grapes
4 cups of water
1 cup of sugar

Slice one cup of grapes, leave the others whole. Toss all the grapes, sugar and water into medium pot. Stir mixture until the sugar has dissolved. Let boil. Remove from heat and let cool. Strain all grape skins from syrup and refrigerate until use.

Peach Cordial

2 cups of Distilled Water
1 cup of White Sugar
1 lb of Fresh Ripe Peaches
2 cups of Vodka (or other Natural Grain Spirit)

Chop peaches into cubes. Add peach cubes, water and sugar to medium saucepan. Cook mixture using medium heat. Stir until smooth. Bring mixture to boil. Add vodka and remove from heat. Let cool. Bottle until use.

Rosemary Syrup

Add 3 cups of water to medium pot. Place on stove and let boil. Delicately place rosemary leaves into water. Add 1½ cups of white sugar. Stir until sugar dissolves. Let steep. Remove from heat. After allowing syrup to cool, pour into jar. Store in the refrigerator until use.

Salting the Rim

Clean and dry glass. Use a slice of citrus to moisten desired area of the glass. Sprinkle salt over moistened area. Carefully tap rocks glass to remove excess salt.

Strawberry Puree

1 ½ cup of Strawberries
1 ½ cup of White Sugar
3 cups of Water

Add 3 cups of water and strawberries to medium pot. Place on stove and let boil. Turn down heat. Add 1.5 cups of white sugar. Stir until sugar dissolves. Bring back to boil. Smash strawberries with muddler to release more juice. Remove from heat. After allowing puree to cool, pour into bottle. Store in the refrigerator until use.

Watermelon Water

Cut open ripe watermelon fruit. Scoop out flesh. In stirring glass, muddle watermelon pieces releasing the juice. Strain into clean bottle. Refrigerate until use.

Terminology

Amaro: Italian herbal liqueur that is commonly consumed as an after-dinner digestif.

Aperitif: An alcoholic drink taken before a meal to stimulate the appetite (example brandy).

Digestif: An alcoholic drink enjoyed in order to aid digestion (example Fernet Branca).

Kolsch: A clear, top-fermented beer with a bright, straw-yellow color. Very similar to a pilsner.

Neat: Spirit served without any additives No ice, sugar — NOTHING.

Pour: Single serving of alcohol.

Spritz: Glass of wine mixed with carbonated water.

Topped: Add liquid until glass is full.

ACKNOWLEDGMENTS

I am forever indebted to my phenomenal mother, Donna Newton, and my always inspiring son, Chance. You two are indeed the anchors and motivating light in my life. Continued appreciation for my mentor, General Hank Taylor, and all of your generous contributions to our cause. May God bless you abundantly. Special thanks to my sister Keva, my brothers Brock and Daniel, and Clay Palmer for believing in me.

Kisses and hugs to every person who liked, shared, commented or even glanced at our blog and social media sites. Thanks to every makeup artist, photographer, graphic designer, intern, bartender, server, hostess, busser and line cook. You make the food and beverage industry possible and our work that much more enjoyable. To all the cabbies, Uber drivers, bus drivers, neighbors, friends and good Samaritans for providing transport, food, financial support and encouraging words to two brown girls with a dream — we thank you! Your support fueled the fire behind this project.

And lastly, to my soul sister and life partner, Taneka Reaves. You are full of love, light and wonder. Never stop imagining, never stop dreaming. Without your spirit, energy and foresight, the Cocktail Bandits would not have existed.

— Johnny

I want to send a sincere thank you to my mother, grandparents and everyone else in my family for all of the support. I hope I'm making you all proud. Also, I have to thank my best friends, Johnny and Marcus, for always believing in me and pushing me to my fullest potential.

Johnny, thank you for everything. Thank you for this amazing journey. Cheers to the next chapter.

— Taneka

Special Thanks To:

Croghan's Jewel Box

West Elm Charleston

Redux Contemporary Art Center

Candy Shop Vintage

Escapada Living

Ashley Raye – MUA

John Mickal – MUA

Katie Fox – MUA

Jada Sanders Nails